TWO PORTRAITS OF ST. THERESE OF LISIEUX

by
ETIENNE ROBO

HENRY REGNERY COMPANY
CHICAGO

Nihil obstat: JEREMIAS J. CURTIN, S.T.D.
CENSOR DEPUTATUS

Imprimatur: HUBERTUS GIBNEY
VIC. GEN.

Southwarci, die 24 Martii, 1955

First published in U.S.A. 1955

ALL RIGHTS RESERVED

MADE AND PRINTED IN GREAT BRITAIN
BY NORTHUMBERLAND PRESS LIMITED
GATESHEAD ON TYNE

St. THÉRÈSE at sixteen

*One of the two photographs taken by Canon Gombault
in Jan. 1889; it has not been touched up.*

CONTENTS

Chapter	Page
INTRODUCTION	9
I. THE FIRST PORTRAIT	17
The popular story of the Little Flower	17
II. THE PHOTOGRAPHS	35
Are they authentic? Prettiness or truth?	35
III. THE SECOND PORTRAIT	47
The realistic approach	47
Childhood and character	49
Teresa's mother's death: a nervous breakdown	52
Innate tendencies: pride and wilfulness. The journey to Rome	64
IV. POSTULANT AND NOVICE	73
First joys and disappointments	73
The Prioress and her Community; the training of the will	80
The forsaking of human affection: A ruthless Teresa	89
Finding herself	98

Chapter	Page
V. A Fully Fledged Carmelite	116
Teresa takes her vows	116
Love one another	118
Companion of Novices	123
Teresa and the Holy Eucharist	125
The "sufferings" of Teresa	127
"My vocation is love"	135
The Little Way	138
VI. The Last Phase	143
Three problems	143
The responsibilities	145
The torment of doubt	154
"I am a saint"	158
Qualis mater, talis filia	173
The last days of Teresa. My God I love Thee	177
Appendix I. Gilding refined gold	189
Appendix II. Style and personality. St. Teresa's Prose and Poems	195

DEDICATION

A la mémoire de ma soeur Marie Louise, religieuse Ursuline, qui mourut de la tuberculose à 26 ans au couvent d'Hennebont en Bretagne en l'année 1904.

INTRODUCTION

OF books on St. Teresa there is no end. They form a stream that continues to flow and swell as the years go by. This shows at least two things: first, that the public interest in the story of this cloistered nun has not vanished, and secondly that, so far, none of the biographies has yet been accepted as conclusive and final. It seems to me that their multiplicity is due less to disagreements concerning facts than to a diversity of interpretations.

Writing as I do in a language not my own I cannot pretend to those gifts of expression that add new charm to an old story. My approach to the subject will perhaps seem new to the Catholic public, for my book is neither a blind panegyric, nor a work of devotion. It is merely a re-statement of the story of St. Teresa made in the detached, objective, and impartial spirit of an historian. This will perhaps contrast strongly with the romantic presentation of novelists, such as *La petite Thérèse* of M. van der Meersch, or the purely edifying ones of uncritical writers; therefore I do not expect it to be welcomed on all sides, and yet I sincerely believe that devotion to St. Teresa is better served by truth than by romance or by pious embellishments. In matters theological I let myself be guided by the teaching of the Church, while in matters of history and of common experience I am the servant of the evidence before me. My opinions may not tally with those of this or that writer; nevertheless I am entitled to formulate the conclusions I arrive at after careful consideration.

Let me make this point clear. I am convinced that the

greatest respect for saints can be reconciled with the truth and even with the criticism of their human weaknesses and oddities. It is not by concealing facts or dressing up the truth that one does them honour. We must not pretend that sanctity alters a man's appearance, endows him with genius, cancels his original inclinations. In fashioning his saints, God makes use of the materials at hand, faulty as He may find them. No hagiographer worthy of the name will pretend it is otherwise. Scripture does not hesitate to inform us that Paul and Barnabas had such differences that they had to part company, that Peter was publicly reproved by Paul and deserved it. Historians inform us that St. Francis Borgia was as round as a barrel and that St. Philip Neri said and did some very odd things. They do not pretend that St. Jerome was meek, St. Francis practical, or the curé d'Ars a genius. Even the writings of the greatest doctors of the Church do not escape criticism.

I cannot see why St. Teresa should be an exception to the rule. I intend to treat her story with the same respect that I would show to the actions and writings of other saints, that is, with well-informed respect and, when there is need for it, a critical respect. I shall not explain away mistakes or indiscretions (should I come across any such) by alleging divine inspiration, nor talk of miracles where natural causes are obviously at work, nor of prophecy when it would be more correct to speak about intelligent foresight.

In adopting this method, I am only following in St. Teresa's footsteps. Once, during her last illness, a nun came and announced to her that, at the moment of death, our Lord accompanied by angels would come to her and she would see them resplendent with light and beauty. She answered, "All these pictures do me no good. I cannot feed on anything but the truth." I might almost say that it is St. Teresa herself who suggested my realistic approach to her biography. A few weeks before her death in the convent infirmary, her mind was dwelling on the story of the Blessed Virgin as it is found in the Gospels. Apart from a few episodes, the sacred

INTRODUCTION 11

writers keep an unbroken silence about the Mother of Christ, in Jerusalem with St. John or at Ephesus—if she ever lived there. This reticence probably means that her everyday life in her poor home was uneventful, and filled up merely with the monotonous, humble tasks of housekeeping. The world saw nothing beyond these deceiving appearances, and Teresa contrasted the reticence of the sacred writers with the fluent inventions of some preachers. These eloquent men, having their own ideas as to what was fitting with, and due to, the dignity of the Mother of God, would in their sermons accumulate privileges, immunities, visions, miracles which left the listeners gasping with "oh's" and "ah's" of admiration. But all these inventions, said Teresa, are untrue and useless. "One is tired of listening to those marvels. They make the Blessed Virgin so different from us ordinary human beings that at the end they raise her as much beyond our love as beyond our imitation. The preachers should tell us of her real life, as the Gospel suggests it, not as they think it *should* have happened."[1]

In short, St. Teresa said: Take your evidence as you find it: do not add to it, do not improve it, use your common sense, not your imagination. This appears to me very sound advice and in writing about her, I shall try to follow it.

Our principal sources of information have been, first of all, the autobiography of St. Teresa herself which Carmel, after a few fumblings, named *The Story of a Soul*; and then *Novissima Verba*, a kind of journal of the last five months of the saint's life, compiled and written by her elder sister Pauline (in religion Mother Agnès de Jesus). We have also consulted other sources, and particularly a voluminous compendium—the work of a team of ten writers—put together by Abbé A. Combes in order to confute, pulverize and annihilate a very brilliant and extremely successful novel by a well-known writer, M. van der Meersch. Novels cannot be expected to square well with history and theology, and the evident admira-

[1] N.V., pp. 117, 147, 154, 158.

tion of the author for St. Teresa has not saved him from mistakes, serious ones in the sight of theologians and historians. Their work of refutation, especially that of Père Noché, throws a good deal of light on life inside the Carmel of Lisieux, and incidentally more light still on the minds of some of the exasperated apologists of St. Teresa who wrote it. If it is true that polemics sometimes disclose the weaknesses of the man who is attacked, it is truer still that they infallibly reveal the character of his critics. Of the adversaries of M. van der Meersch I can say that one was as courteous as he was witty, another showed partiality without being aware of it, and one or two . . . perhaps I had better leave it at that. It is enough to say that religious controversies often lack the most important and the sweetest element of Religion, which is Charity. Their book is called: *La petite Sainte Thérèse de M. van der Meersch devant la critique et devant les textes.* We shall refer to it by the letter "C", in the same manner as we shall refer to the English translation of *The Story of a Soul* by the letter "E". This able version is the work of Mgr. Thomas N. Taylor and is widely known. This will enable my readers to verify the accuracy of my quotations of *The Story of a Soul.* To *Novissima Verba* I have allotted the letters, "N.V.". The book of Père Petitot, to which I refer sometimes, is his *Ste. Thérèse de Lisieux*, final edition.

I am in a difficulty regarding *The Story of a Soul.* No one denies that the text before the public, up to now, has been edited, curtailed, arranged, corrected to some extent, how far we do not know, though Abbé Combes assures us that the result is exactly what Teresa herself would have wished. As one who has for years worked on original manuscripts, I must be forgiven if I maintain that no historical documents should ever be tampered with; I refuse absolutely to accept good intentions as a valid excuse for so-called "improvements". I rejoice over the intended publication of the manuscript in photostat form, as, no doubt, it will dispose of many unpleasant rumours, fostered by the incomprehensible opposition to this step from some quarters.

Meanwhile, I have to work on the only text I possess, correct or not. I should like to point out that the mistakes, the unguarded expressions, the many *lapsus calami* of an author who has had no time to revise his work, are often more revealing, more illuminating than a corrected text and for this reason should be preserved.[2] I believe, however, that the publication of the original manuscript will, if anything, confirm, not invalidate, my conclusions.

My quotations of the *Summarium* are, all of them, at second hand; for I have not had direct access to the evidence collected in view of the Process of canonization. In his informative book, *La réponse des textes et des archives*, Père A. Noché, S.J., gives more than 200 quotations from that source and in Mr. J. Beevers' book, *Storm of Glory*, I found a few more which do not show the Prioress, M. de Gonzague, in a very favourable light. These seem to have escaped the attention of Père Noché. I wish to acknowledge here my debt to both these writers, and the use I have made of their quotations. I hold that in order to help the readers to form a balanced judgment of any public or historical character, the historian has the right and duty to produce all the evidence, pleasant and less pleasant, that has come within his knowledge.

I must express my gratitude here to various friends who have encouraged me in pursuing my work and particularly to the one who agreed to edit this little book and also to correct the proofs. My failing eyesight would have made this a difficult task and I am grateful to him.

[2] To give an instance of this: a fragment of the 17th chapter of St. John's Gospel quoted by Teresa appears in both English and French texts of *L'Histoire d'une âme* (French edition 1900 and 1953) but is more complete in the English version than in the French. It might be thought of no importance, but the verses omitted in the French text are precisely such as would throw a vivid light on Teresa's theory of her own sanctity. As I have not had access to the first French edition of 1897-8 I cannot suggest which rendering is the original one, but the question does not lack interest.

FIRST PORTRAIT

CHAPTER I

THE FIRST PORTRAIT

THE POPULAR STORY OF THE LITTLE FLOWER

To the English public at large, the name of St. Teresa of Lisieux means little or nothing. Generally speaking, Catholics are but dimly acquainted with her story and, among her most enthusiastic devotees, not more than five per cent have attempted to read a few pages of her autobiography, *The Story of a Soul*, while not one in a hundred has read it carefully from cover to cover. Before putting into their hands my own critical version of that story, it may be advisable to recapitulate it briefly in the form it came to them previously, in sermons or popular tracts. This I shall do without offering my own comments of approval or disapproval. It will refresh their memory and allow them later on to see clearly where my own account diverges from the purely edifying and uncritical renderings with which they are familiar.

Teresa wrote the first part of her autobiography at the command of Pauline, her sister, then Prioress of the Carmel of Lisieux. At this time she was nearly twenty-two. Three-quarters of it are devoted to her childhood and here is an appreciation of this part of the work.

"Among her pages of rare beauty, few are more beautiful than those which afford a glimpse into the home of her parents, Louis Martin and Zélie Guérin. They rival sometimes the finest French prose."[1]

At the beginning of her story Teresa underlined the religious atmosphere of her family, for she fully realized the all-decisive influence this had had on her spiritual formation. Long before they thought of marriage, both her parents had seriously

[1] E, pp. 16, 25.

considered embracing the religious life and they kept to the end the fervent religious outlook with which they had begun. Teresa was the last of nine children that were born to them, only five of whom, all girls, came to maturity, and one after another entered convents.

Even before Teresa was born, it was felt by her mother that she was no ordinary child. During her time of waiting, Mme. Martin had an uncommon experience. In a letter addressed to her sister-in-law, she says that, unbelievable as it sounds, she could hear the voice of the unborn infant, "When I sang, she sang with me."[2] Whatever explanation we offer of this prodigy, we cannot doubt that the grace of God was at work from the beginning. As Dom Artus puts it: "Before the baby was capable of making a single act of will, God had predestined it to the highest sanctity."[3] In the soil where she grew she was preserved from the poisoned breath of the world until the good master transplanted her to the mountain of Carmel. In this truly Christian family, the conversation was of holy things; their daily life was regulated by the love of God, and by religious observances. Even the games of the children had often a religious connotation. Teresa was able to say that from the age of three she had never refused God anything. At four she thought, "I will be a nun." The first word she could read alone was "Heaven". "See, Father," she said one evening, looking at a cluster of stars, "here is a 'T', my name is written in heaven." At five she follows perfectly a sermon on the Passion, and at six, one Sunday evening after Compline, "she felt like an exile on this earth. I longed for the repose of heaven, the never-ending sabbath of our true home." In short, from her tenderest infancy, her thoughts were already fixed on the invisible world, not on the vanities of this present life.

When she was four years and a half, her mother died, but, such was the control she had at this tender age over her emotions, grief-stricken as she was, she shed no tears and

[2] *Histoire d'une famille* by Fr. Stephané J. Piat, O.F.M.
[3] C, p. 232.

THE FIRST PORTRAIT

remained apparently unmoved. It had been a very great shock and from that day she became timid and shy and strangely sensitive, whereas before she had been lively and demonstrative. She was devoted to her sister Pauline and from then onwards always called her "her little mother" and loved and obeyed her as if she had been her real mother.

Five years later she suffered another great shock. Pauline left her and entered Carmel. For the second time, she had become an orphan. "I could not understand this and my heart cried out: 'Pauline is lost to me.'"

About this time, Teresa, who was then nearly ten years old, began to suffer from constant and severe headaches and this was followed by an extraordinary and mysterious illness, most probably not due entirely to natural causes,[4] the work of the Evil One. She seemed to be delirious most of the time, and was often in a state of catalepsy and yet she could see and hear everything that was going on round her. She remained conscious and was never deprived of her reason. Humanly speaking there was no hope of recovery. God allowed evil spirits to approach her bed of sickness and to frighten her by terrifying hallucinations. Prayers, novenas, Masses seemed to remain unanswered. At last a miracle put a sudden end to the long trial. As Marie and Céline were praying on their knees in front of a statue of the Virgin in the bedroom, the statue was seen by Teresa to come to life. The radiant and beautiful apparition took a step towards her and smiled, while the child, transfigured and with a rapt expression on her face, was watching. She was cured, and all her life the memory of that smile haunted her.[5]

She remained, however, very sensitive. She had always wept easily since her mother's death, and this tendency grew worse as years went on. She says herself that she often cried without reason except because she had cried. This sensitive-

[4] C, p. 289. Note 12.
[5] For a full account read the Autobiography and the footnote signed: Carmel. Also C, p. 70: "... the strange illness followed by such a conspicuous and miraculous cure".

ness was great, says Père Noché, S.J., "but not excessive",[6] and there is no proof that her tears were considered a nuisance by the household. The reason for her tears, continues the good Jesuit, was the fear of having displeased God, or having caused some pain to her father.[7]

This weakness was at last cured by what is considered to have been a miracle. She was very nearly fourteen when it happened on Christmas night in 1886, and it steered her spiritual life for ever on the road of complete self-forgetfulness. Before starting for the Midnight Mass, Teresa had laid her shoes in front of the hearth as she had always done, that on her return she might find them filled with sweets and little presents. On her return from church, as she was going up to her room, she overheard her father say, "All this is far too babyish for a big girl like Teresa, I hope this is the last time it will happen." On hearing this, Teresa was about to burst into tears as usual, when Céline came and begged her to wait a few minutes and compose herself before going downstairs. All of a sudden Jesus transformed her and she was able to master herself and to join the others with a smiling face. "The fountain of my tears was dried up," writes Teresa, "and from that day they flowed neither easily nor often. On that night, the sweet Infant Jesus flooded with His glorious sunshine the darkness in which my soul was plunged and made me strong and brave. From then on I went on from victory to victory, beginning, so to speak, to run like a giant."[8]

This does not mean that she ceased afterwards to feel acutely the many trials and disappointments of her life. She remained very sensitive but mastered herself to this extent, that no one afterwards was aware of the many sufferings she went through. "Her capacity to suffer was a special grace, in fact an answer to the prayers with which Jesus inspired her during a thanksgiving after Holy Communion in 1889."[9]

---

[6] C, pp. 290-1.
[7] My tears "flowed for the most trivial cause . . . I would cry for having cried". E, pp. 83-84.
[8] E, pp. 86-87.   [9] C, p. 290.

Those who knew her during this period of her short life have left us their impressions in the evidence they sent to Rome for the canonization. Her sisters, a servant, one of the school mistresses and others, speak of her in the following terms:

"Vanity was unknown to her; she was indifferent to dress and never used perfume; she did not know she was pretty and did not use a looking glass without necessity. She never pushed herself forward and always avoided compliments—she was always simple and humble; she truly believed herself inferior to others—she was perfectly well balanced and her will was in complete command of her faculties—always patient and of an even disposition, she was never known to show any temper. She was very docile and, if she made some little slip, it was enough for her parents to express disapproval and she never again repeated it. She was very pious, very gentle, of an exemplary goodness (*sagesse*, i.e. not getting into mischief as all children do)."[10] A former servant testifies she was always very cheerful, and Marie adds: "She appeared to me, from her earliest childhood, as an angel that God had sent into the world in a mortal body."[11] This is how her sisters and others remembered Teresa a quarter of a century after her death.

The reason she gave for entering Carmel was that she had come to save souls by prayer and suffering. At an early age she had already devoted herself to prayer for sinners. Hearing that a notorious criminal, Pranzini, was to be executed, and showed no signs of repentance, she set herself to win him by her prayers to God. She felt quite sure they would be answered, but nevertheless she begged our Lord for a sign. When she opened the newspaper announcing the execution, she saw that the poor man, as he was being dragged to the guillotine, suddenly turned to the priest, seized his crucifix and kissed our Lord's sacred wounds three times. She had had the sign she wanted.

At the age of eight she was sent to school to a Benedictine

---

[10] See C, pp. 290, 292. [11] C, p. 294.

convent in the neighbourhood of Lisieux. She was younger than her schoolfellows, but very studious, and did not share school games. Add to this that she was shy and sensitive, and we can see why she does not seem to have been very popular, and why she was not successful in making friends. She remarked that this failure of hers in winning the affection of girls and mistresses "saved her from many evils and she was thankful to our Lord that He allowed her to find only bitterness in earthly friendships".[12] It was about that time that she prayed our Lord "to turn into bitterness for her all the consolations of the world".

She was not happy in the convent, and for reasons of health M. Martin took her away to finish her education at home.

She had always wanted to be a nun, and at the age of nine had confided her secret to the Prioress of the Carmelites in Lisieux. She received words of encouragement, but it was explained to her that she could not be accepted before the age of sixteen. At about fourteen, she felt unable to wait any longer; she must enter Carmel before Christmas of that year (1887) that is just before the age of fifteen. This was no doubt an effect of divine inspiration, yet to her great sorrow one difficulty arose after another. Her father, it is true, gave his consent readily, but Marie, her elder sister, disagreed with her, and her uncle, Isidore Guérin, strongly disapproved of what he considered to be an imprudent step. Opposition arose from one quarter after another. Canon Delatroëtte, the ecclesiastical superior of Carmel, put his veto upon her reception until she was twenty-one, and although the Bishop of Bayeux, Mgr. Hugonin, spoke to her kindly when she called on him with her father, he did not seem to take very seriously this girl of fourteen who wept so easily and wanted to become a Carmelite perhaps before she could realize the seriousness of such a step.

She wept on this occasion, as she wept each time her desires, or rather the evident will of God—was not recognized, yet

[12] E, p. 78.

in her heart always "reigned a wonderful peace because she was seeking only God's will".[13]

We must here call attention to a singular coincidence—if it is a coincidence—which Teresa notes carefully after an interview with her uncle Guérin when she had shed many tears. "Nature seemed to share my deep sadness; during those three days of despair there was not a ray of sunshine and the rain fell in torrents. Again and again I have noticed that all through my life nature has reflected my feelings. When I wept the heavens wept with me; when I rejoiced no cloud darkened the azure sky."

At the end of their unsuccessful interview with the bishop, M. Martin had announced his intention of taking his daughter to Rome in order to appeal to the Holy Father himself and obtain the permission which had been refused at Lisieux. This journey took place in November 1887 when they joined a diocesan pilgrimage to Rome.

At the papal audience, as they were already kneeling in front of the Pope, the Vicar General of Bayeux, aware of Teresa's intentions, announced in a loud voice that he absolutely forbade anyone to address the Holy Father. Céline, at her elbow, said to her sister: "Speak", and in obedience to God's command, her eyes blinded with tears, she implored the Pope to allow her to enter Carmel at fifteen. Leo XIII referred her to her superiors, adding, "Child, you will enter if it be God's will." Teresa, who knew that she was seeking God's will, was going to insist and, her hand on the Pope's knees, refused to obey the Noble Guards who came and bade her rise. They had to take her by the arms, lift her to her feet and remove her weeping out of the room.[14] Her sorrow was crushing, her heart was pierced and "the beautiful Italian sky mingled its tears unceasingly with mine".[15]

This courageous perseverance, which led her from Lisieux to Bayeux and from Bayeux to Rome, was not obstinacy. She was acting under divine guidance. Even at the Vatican she showed no disobedience, but, as Père Noché explains it, "only

[13] E, p. 102.   [14] E, p. 114.   [15] C, p. 298.

great energy, but energy in the service of a divine will that was evident. She did not hesitate, because there was no reason why she should."[16] This was neither defiance nor obstinacy. "It was," says Dom Artus, O.S.B., "the confident answer of a little girl to the Voice of Him who was in fact the Highest, and who demands everything from His creatures."[17] For this reason Teresa paid no attention to the obstacles she met.

There were new delays. The bishop gave his consent in January, and the Prioress of Carmel put off the reception as postulant for another three months.

She entered Carmel on April 9th, 1888. Some unexpected trials awaited her. The Prioress, formerly so friendly, now treated her with unexpected severity, not because of any dislike for Teresa, whose virtues she was one of the first to perceive, but in order to prove her, to subdue her pride, and advance her in the ways of perfection. The young girl realized it and thanked God for sending her such a sound and valuable training. In her biography, she always speaks of the Prioress with the greatest affection and gratitude. "You are the compass which Jesus has provided me, to direct me safely to the eternal shore."[18]

She speaks lovingly of the Prioress—then seriously ill—when she writes to Céline, who had not yet entered Carmel: "It is so sad to see the people we love suffer. Although Jesus is very desirous to enjoy in heaven the presence of our darling (*chérie*) Mother, He cannot refuse to leave with us the one whose motherly hand knows so well how to lead us and to console us in this life's exile."[19] In an earlier letter still: "How good is Jesus to have given us a Mother such as the one we have."

At the same time she experienced great aridity, that is, a complete absence of consolation and comfort in her devotions and in the practices of religious life. These two trials she

[16] C, p. 298.   [17] C, p. 239.   [18] E, p. 161.
[19] Letter CVIII, p. 190, quoted by A. Noché, S.J.

accepted with joy and offered them to Jesus for the salvation of souls. "Suffering opened wide her arms to me from the first and I took her fondly to my heart."[20] She does not seem to have found much help in the confessional. She had always had the greatest difficulty in opening her heart to her confessor. For one thing she was troubled with scruples, and, as everybody knows, these are as much of a trial to confessors as they are to penitents. They may not have shown her as much patience and sympathy as she expected. As a result, it is true to say that she never had any spiritual director except Jesus Himself. Under His divine guidance, "gradually the little flower unfolded itself under the shadow of the Cross". On two occasions only did she find in confessors the understanding and encouragement needed to follow freely the inspirations of grace. One of them was Père Pichon, S.J. Astonished at the workings of grace he discovered in her and marvelling at so great a holiness in so young a girl—she was then a little over fifteen—he exclaimed after her general confession, "Before God, the Blessed Virgin, the Angels and all the Saints, I declare that you have never committed a mortal sin." This man, concluded Teresa, combined knowledge with virtue and "seemed to me to come from God Himself".[21]

She made her profession on September 8th, 1890. On the eve of the great day, "the devil—for it was he—assured her that she was wholly unsuited for the Carmelite life".[22] The devil was, however, put to instant flight after she had told the novice mistress of her temptation. She was never troubled again in this manner and pronounced her holy vows with a soul flooded with heavenly joy.

Of her life in the convent there is little to say in the way of external events. Her fights, her victories in the spiritual order, were largely hidden from the eyes of others. After her death, when the question of canonization was raised, not a few of her companions remembered that she had always been admired for her fidelity to the rules and looked upon as a saint. Her own sister Pauline stated that the nuns had for her

[20] E, p. 123. [21] E, p. 124. [22] E, p. 135.

an esteem and a veneration they had for no one else. Sister Aimée de Jésus declared before the Roman Tribunal that while the Servant of God was still alive, even at the time when she took the veil, but more so during the last period of her life, she "was looked upon in the community as a little saint. This was our general opinion." Pauline adds: "The Sisters who most of them expected an ordinary child, were, so to speak, seized with respect in her presence. There was in her person something so dignified, modest and resolute that I was surprised myself." Her former novice mistress expresses herself in terms more emphatic still: "From the beginning, the Servant of God astonished the community by her conduct marked with a kind of majesty. They were far from expecting this."[23] Sister Marie de la Trinité had even on one occasion fallen on her knees to her and said: "I am sure that after your death they will go on their knees and say, Saint Teresa of the Infant Jesus, pray for us." A few were perhaps at first less discerning but were soon unanimous in recognizing her eminent sanctity. Externally, apart from her meticulous observance of the rules there was nothing very noticeable about her, but this was entirely due to her perfect humility. During the first two years she was given a number of menial tasks, mending linen, sweeping passages, the stairs, a dormitory and the refectory. Once, perhaps a year after her entrance, she was cleaning the chapel with some other novices, when the following incident took place which shows her simple faith and devotion to the Holy Eucharist. One of her companions saw her kneel and then, rising, knock at the door of the tabernacle and ask, "Art Thou there, Jesus? I beseech Thee to speak to me."[24] And she stayed for some seconds with her head against the tabernacle.

She received the veil and took her vows in September 1890. The following year she was given the office of sacristan. She had to take care of the altar and prepare the vestments and chalice for the Mass. Nothing could have given her greater joy than the handling of the altar linen and of the sacred

[23] Petitot, p. 46.   [24] *Storm of Glory*, John Beevers, p. 119.

THE FIRST PORTRAIT

vessels for it made her feel she was taking an active part in the Holy Sacrifice. She took a childish delight in seeing her own reflection in the shining surface of paten and chalice and she kissed not only the corporals on which the body of the Lord would rest, but even the large host that was to be consecrated.

At the end of the same year an epidemic of influenza claimed many victims in the community and a few of the Sisters died. Teresa helped in the care of the sick. Later on she was asked by the former Prioress, now Mistress of Novices, to share with her the task of looking after the five novices. This was an unofficial post, but she discharged her duties in an exemplary manner, and thanks to her great tact managed to avoid scenes with Mother Marie de Gonzague, who was sometimes difficult. Her novices—they were not yet perfect, and Teresa could be stern—did not always accept her admonitions meekly. Her love for them was very real, but unmixed with human and selfish elements, and when necessary, she never feared a conflict. At the end "her little lambs", as she called them, realized that her reprimands were always inspired by true charity. Teresa confesses that sometimes she could read their thoughts so clearly that it gave her "an impression of the supernatural" and that she spoke "as one inspired".[25]

This gift of second sight was not the only remarkable endowment she possessed. Her prayers were often answered in a way that was almost uncanny. She asked for signs and obtained them. At one time it happened that, when Communion was given at Mass, the priest having too few consecrated Hosts left in the ciborium had to divide them, and this, having been repeated for a few mornings, Teresa was afraid it might mean that our Lord did not want to come to her. She asked for a sign and lo! that very next morning, the priest by mistake gave her two Hosts instead of one. She herself had noticed years before that nature reflected her feelings. This is what actually happened when she took the

[25] E, pp. 180-1.

veil. She had long wished to see the earth covered with snow on this day, when she herself would be dressed like a bride in pure white velvet. The weather (it was January 10th) was mild and no one could have expected to see this wish realized. But when she set foot in the enclosure and turned to the inner court, she saw it was all covered with snow; in order "to gratify the least wish of His little spouse He actually made her a gift of the snow ".[26] Everyone was so amazed that since then they have described that event as "the little miracle".

Teresa ever disclaimed having had visions or revelations and went so far as to say that she did not wish for these favours,[27] but, in a conversation with Pauline, revealed that once when in chapel starting the Stations of the Cross she felt herself wounded as by a burning shaft so that she felt like dying. It was as if she had been plunged into a furnace by an invisible hand. "Oh! what a fire and what sweetness at the same time. . . . It happened only once and for one single instant and then my ordinary state of aridity returned."[28]

We must speak here of an extraordinary privilege which Père Petitot in his *Sainte Thérèse de Lisieux* seems to consider authentic. The saint—it was in June 1895—offered herself as a victim to the justice of God on behalf of sinners, consenting to suffer punishment in their stead. She wrote this in the form of a prayer of dedication and at the end of it expressed the daring wish that she might become the living tabernacle where our Lord would remain permanently present. As far as is known she never explained to anyone what she meant, but her sister Pauline certifies that she herself is certain that Teresa had in mind the miraculous permanence of the Host, and that her wish was granted.

For a little time after her arrival, encouraged perhaps by the zealous Prioress, she tried to emulate some of the unusual bodily penances of the saints, but soon it became evident to her that out-of-the-way, self-imposed, physical macerations were not for her. "One should practise them with great moderation," she said. "They are more often inspired by

[26] E, p. 129.   [27] N.V., p. 177.   [28] N.V., pp. 52-53.

human motives than by the love of God."[29] She held, as do the masters of the spiritual life, that mortification of one's will, of one's pride, of one's affections are more effective than long fasts and scourgings. In the long run she saw clearly that very small acts of renunciation, constantly repeated, can lead to God as surely as more spectacular deeds, on condition they are completely free from personal motives and done or accepted entirely for the love of God. "Love," she said, " is the only thing that counts." " God has no need of our good works, she repeated; what He wants is uniquely (*uniquement*) our love."[30]

From the very start she kept every rule strictly, minutely, constantly. She never asked for exemptions, and not only did she never complain of the food although the vegetarian diet did not suit her at all, but she did not even seem to notice what she was eating. She suffered intensely from cold during the winter months. It was only on her death-bed that she even mentioned it to her sister. She obeyed the ringing of the bell as if it were the voice of God. She never put herself forward, never argued, and submitted without protest to every reproof, even an unjust one. Remember that she was naturally full of pride, as the Prioress explained once to Pauline in order to justify her severities.

She was very fond of her sisters, but until she became ill and almost helpless, she kept them at a distance, and treated Pauline, whom she had loved best, as a complete stranger. This act of self-sacrifice must have been particularly difficult to one of such an affectionate nature as Teresa.

In her autobiography she gives some instances of her little victories. Once she accepted in silence an undeserved reprimand about a broken jar for which somebody else was responsible. She refrained from complaining when a pretty little jug was removed from her cell and replaced by an old

---

[29] N.V., p. 110.
[30] E, p. 198, and French text, p. 163, ed. 1953. M. van der Meersch seems to have taken this saying so literally that he was much misled by it.

one, chipped all over, or when her lamp was taken from the shelf by mistake and she had to sit in the dark for one hour. Such mortifications as these are small things, but you will notice that all of them were of the kind that made life easier for others. She would smile to people who got on her nerves, pretend to herself that the irritating jangle of rosaries was sweet music. She bore kindly, almost tenderly, with the old and crotchety. There is great virtue in all such small sacrifices.

Like some illustrious Doctors of the Church, Teresa left to the world as a kind of spiritual testament a "completely new doctrine" to lead souls to perfection. It has been hailed as an important original contribution to spiritual literature, and Dom Artus, O.S.B., goes so far as to say "her doctrine of the Little Way has been in some degree canonized at the same time as St. Teresa herself".[31]

She attached the greatest importance to this new doctrine which she called *The Little Way* and a few weeks before her death spoke of the good it would do to souls. Her mission after death, she said, would be to spread the knowledge of her "Little Way".[32] It was specially addressed to those whom she calls the "little souls", to those who live in ordinary, unimportant circumstances. She praised the value of every trivial action performed for the love of God and compares them to flowers that are thrown at the feet of Jesus, useless perhaps but beautiful. Since little souls are aware of their own insignificance and weakness, they must throw themselves in the arms of Jesus, which, like a lift, will carry them without effort to the summits of perfection. The "Little Way" is one of trust in God and absolute surrender. "To attain true holiness, it is enough to humble oneself and bear meekly with one's own imperfections."[33]

Let us add as a corrective that Teresa not only held that good works were necessary, but by her own life, her struggles

---

[31] C, p. 228.
[32] N.V., pp. 79, 81.
[33] Letters, p. 406. This, again, is perhaps the text which led M. van der Meersch astray.

and her victories proved that she did not think that sentiment was all-sufficient.

The disease that was to carry her away revealed itself in April 1896 during Holy Week after Teresa had kept rigorously the austerities of Lent. During the night of Holy Thursday to Good Friday, and the following night as well, she had hæmorrhages of the lung. She told the Prioress of it as she was bound to do, but nobody else. She herself, however, was well aware of her condition and wrote: "I was firmly convinced that on the anniversary of His death my Beloved had allowed me to hear His first call, like a sweet distant murmur, heralding His joyful approach."[34]

Some writers tell us that this illness was an answer to prayer. In June 1895 she had offered herself as a victim to the justice of God, taking upon herself the punishment due to sinners. "It seems," she writes, "that if Thou shouldst find souls offering themselves as a holocaust to Thy Love, Thou wouldst consume them rapidly and wouldst be pleased to set free those flames of infinite tenderness now imprisoned in Thy Heart." "O Jesus, permit that I may be that happy victim—consume Thy holocaust with the fire of Divine Love."[35]

Dom Artus makes the following comment: "The illness of Teresa followed immediately on the act of oblation.[36] Was it not God's answer to this magnanimous offering? Is not God free to use His absolute rights over His consenting creature? Might not Teresa's illness be one of those co-redeeming painful complaints, the causes and cure of which are beyond the power of man, like the stigmata of St. Francis and the sores of St. Lydwine. She had had prophetical warnings of her early death."[37]

There have been some allegations of neglect against the Prioress, because for one year—that is until April 1897—her complaint received no treatment worth mentioning. No one

---

[34] E, p. 154.   [35] E, p. 148.
[36] We should note, however, that the first signs of her illness had already appeared nearly two years earlier, in 1894. See C, pp. 391-2.
[37] C, p. 250.

in the convent, not even the Prioress, knew that Teresa was ill. In their deposition for the Tribunal in Rome the Sisters have been unanimous on this point, and if their impressions of what the doctor said are correct, even Dr. de Cornières had not the slightest notion of the nature of the disease until a few weeks before Teresa died. The Prioress spoke of her with admiration, called her the angel of the house, and Teresa herself testifies to the attention and good nursing she was given as soon as it was discovered she was ill. "Your devotedness throughout my illness, dear Reverend Mother, has taught me many a lesson of charity. No remedy seems too costly, and should one fail, you try something else. . . . What precautions you take to protect me from the slightest draught."[38]

During the last two years of her life, a new trial, this one of a spiritual nature, rent her heart. It was the worst of all the storms she had passed through, and the most distressing. This was the temptation of religious doubt, her final and greatest test, but from the start she knew it for what it was, a temptation. "God allowed my own soul to be plunged in the deepest gloom and the thought of heaven to become a subject of torture. . . . I lack the consolations of faith but I live as if I had it. I have made more acts of faith during the past year than in all the rest of my life." Père Noché, S.J., gives the following explanation: "The saint had lost the feeling of certainty, but not the certainty which faith is. . . . This is why she could write: 'And so during this long trial Thou hast given me, O Lord, a delight in Thy doings, for is there a greater joy than to suffer for Thy love, O my God.'"[39] We can say that not only was there peace, but even joy in her soul in the midst of her temptations.

Her physical sufferings were great, her agony prolonged, but her patience was admirable, and to the end she greeted with a smile anyone who came near her.

During the last weeks of her illness, many remarkable sayings of hers were piously recorded by her sister Pauline who,

[38] E, p. 182.   [39] E, p. 157.

as well as Marie and Céline, was constantly in attendance in the infirmary on Teresa. They were even occasionally taken under dictation, and assembled together in a little book called *Novissima Verba*, i.e. *Last Words*. Some of her best-known sayings are known now all over the world, "I will spend my heaven in doing good upon earth", "After my death I will send down a shower of roses", "All the world will love me". In the presence of her three sisters she even said: "You know well that you are nursing a little saint." In view of what has happened after her death it is impossible to deny her a gift of prophecy. Not only did she foresee her own canonization, but Pauline tells us that during her illness she had affirmed that the weather would be fine at the hour of her death.[40]

During the last days of her illness, birds came and sang for her as she lay in bed. On one occasion there was a linnet and a canary; on another, the day before her death, a dove lighted on the window-sill, cooing there for a considerable time, a thing that had never happened before. Pauline and Céline, deeply moved, recalled the words of the Song of Songs (II, 10, 11, 12): "The voice of the turtle dove is heard in the land. . . . Arise, my love . . . my beautiful one and come."

At length her heroic patience and love were to have their reward. Her agony began on September 30th at about 4 p.m. "I should not have thought it possible to suffer so much," she said, "I can only explain it by my intense desire to save souls." And later: "I do not regret having surrendered myself to love."

Soon after seven o'clock the end came. She had just been told that her suffering might yet be prolonged for some hours and she had answered, "Very well . . . be it so . . . I do not wish to suffer less," when, looking at her crucifix, she continued: "Oh! I love Him. My God, I love Thee."

These were her last words. "Scarcely had she spoken when her whole frame drooped suddenly, the head inclined a little to the right in the attitude of the Virgin martyrs offering themselves to the sword; or rather as a victim of love, await-

[40] N.V., p. 199.

ing from the divine Archer the fiery shaft by which she longs to die. Then, raising herself as though called by a mysterious voice and opening her eyes which shone with unutterable joy, she fixed her gaze a little above the statue of the Virgin facing her bed and then her blessed soul, the prey of the 'Divine Eagle', was borne away to the heights of heaven."[41]

She had promised a shower of roses. And even before she was buried, "there began to occur in the convent certain extraordinary incidents of which the following may be mentioned as examples. The first is that of a lay Sister who on kissing the feet of the Servant of God was instantly cured of cerebral anaemia. A child of ten was favoured with a strong perfume of lilies and a nun with that of violets; while a third felt herself thrilled by a kiss bestowed on her by some invisible being. One Sister perceived a bright light in the heavens, and another saw a luminous crown which, rising from the earth, was soon lost in space."[42]

These occurrences were only a beginning, for many are the favours of every kind she has obtained for her clients since that day. The translator of *The Story of a Soul*, Mgr. Thomas N. Taylor, rightly calls them "a riot of roses in June" and assures us that "God will refuse nothing in Paradise to her who refused Him nothing on earth: that she will continue her work from heaven until the last soul has entered its gates".

[41] E, p. 240. In Appendix I, the reader will find a criticism of these poetical effusions as well as our comments on the incidents mentioned in the paragraph which follows.
[42] E, p. 241.

CHAPTER II

THE PHOTOGRAPHS

PRETTINESS OR TRUTH?

IN the preceding chapter we have drawn the portrait of St. Teresa as it can be found in various books written with the sole purpose of edifying the reader or glorifying the saint. Such a purpose could not be expected to fit in at all points with historical evidence. Before drawing a second version of the character and personality of Teresa—one more consonant with the facts—it is relevant to warn the reader that her physical appearance has also undergone a parallel treatment of idealization. We might even add that, until the manuscript of her autobiography has been published in photostat, there will remain some doubt whether its text has, or has not, been tampered with in the same manner and with the same pious intentions as her lives and portraits.

The photographs have been touched up, rectified, improved, beautified, call it what you like, by her sister Céline, who had a gift for painting, until their resemblance to the original became merely a matter of opinion. This beauty-parlour treatment is no longer denied. Carmel admits it and tries to minimize and to justify it. One can read their explanations in a booklet issued by them, *A propos des portraits de S. Thérèse de l'Enfant Jésus,* and in our judgment they tend rather to obscure the problem than to solve it. Some of the text seems to be due to the pen of Mother Agnès (13th page), and the introductory note is from that of a *Vicaire Général,* P. Th. Dubosq. This note is a reprint of an official communication from the bishop's house (Semaine religieuse, 12 Sept. 1915), concerning a portrait of the saint which appeared on the front page of the big edition of *Histoire d'une Ame.* "This," it says, "is a very conscientious and carefully studied synthesis of the best elements offered by the many untouched photographs at the disposal of Carmel."

The discerning public remained unimpressed and unconvinced by this declaration of 1915, and eleven years later P. Th. Dubosq, V.G., repeated it in his foreword to the little booklet inspired or written by Mother Agnès, then Prioress of Carmel. It concedes that "some photographs were slightly altered by Céline in order to give them the right expression". "Compare them," it says, "with the uncorrected and unauthorized prints; do you not agree that the first gives us the better average resemblance to the saint?"

What a question! How could we tell? How could we agree? What is an *average* resemblance to an original we have never seen? This is very perplexing, and more so when the synthetic result is put forward and sworn to as the authentic portrait of the saint. What do they mean by "authentic"? No one denies the photographs have undergone many transformations and they could only be authentic in an impressionist sense. It is Teresa as, after many years, the Sisters think they remember her, or, shall we say, wish to remember her. Such a trick of memory is not uncommon. Relations keep in their mind—and on their mantelpiece—an idealized or rejuvenated picture of a dear departed because it corresponds unconsciously to their wishes, if not to reality. Who has not come across some lively examples of this little weakness? We, the general public, may be permitted however to investigate the facts a bit further. The powerful means of publicity at the disposal of the Carmel of Lisieux has made it hard for criticism to make itself heard. The "synthetic" pictures are on sale everywhere, while the untouched photographs seldom reach the public. They try to discredit the few that are still procurable, and one is further handicapped when describing and criticizing their revised versions of St. Teresa's face by the fact that they are copyright and one cannot publish them side by side with the originals for the sake of comparison. We have been refused permission to reproduce here their postcard of Teresa as a novice at the age of sixteen. This refusal is an answer. They dare not face the comments of the public when they see side by side the original and the fake.

Since Carmel agrees that there has been some manipulation of the photographs, only two questions are before us. One is of degree: how far have the "improvements" altered the originals? Secondly: is it permissible to correct original documents concerning public characters?

The early portraits may not be of much interest to the general reader. We may note that even the earliest one—Teresa, age $3\frac{1}{2}$ years[1]—has been slightly rectified. (Note of P. Th. Dubosq.) Curiously enough it bears no resemblance to the painting of Teresa with her mother by Céline, presumably at about the same time, since Teresa was only $4\frac{1}{2}$ years when her mother died. In this painting the round full face of the child has been elongated by Céline. It is the same process that we find at work on later pictures and makes us wonder whether Céline suffered from astigmatism.

We have seen side by side two unmounted photographs of Teresa (aged 8) with her sister Céline, both of them from the same negative. (There was quite a story attached to these pictures.) In the improved copy, not only had they reconstituted a big silk bow which was merely indicated in the other—this, of course, is quite justifiable—but a new supply of hair had been piled up on the head of the child and the line of the mouth had also been altered. The uncorrected version appears in J. Beevers' *Storm of Glory*, and the corrected one in Père S. Piat's *Histoire d'une famille*. In an actual photographic print—an untouched one—which was lent to the author, the differences between the original and the corrected pictures are more evident than in the book illustrations. These two examples of rectification do not amount to much and were they standing alone would not be worth remarking upon. They only indicate a general wish to improve on nature.

[1] The French edition of *Histoire d'une âme* (1953) says three, but Pauline's booklet says three and a half years.

The photograph that appears on the cover of this book shows Teresa at sixteen. It was taken by Abbé Gombault (later on Canon Gombault) then Procurator of the Junior Seminary at Lisieux. At that time he was also diocesan inspector of religious buildings in the diocese and had to report to the bishop on their condition. We have to specify this because the French text of Mother Agnès in *A propos des portraits* reads as if Abbé Gombault had no good reason to enter the monastery. (*Entré exceptionellement au Monastère pour un " tout autre motif "*.)

Here is the story of this photograph as we heard it from people who knew him well. On one occasion when he had come to the convent on an official mission he happened to have brought his camera and was asked to take a photo of Teresa, a new novice just sixteen years old. He kept the negative and for the time being did not give another thought to it. A few years later it began to be rumoured that Teresa might be canonized and many people asked him for copies of his picture which, as he soon found out, no longer agreed with Céline's idea of what a saint should look like. The bishop was asked by the convent to retrieve the "unfaithful" negative from the possession of Abbé Gombault. Not overpleased at being deprived of his property, this priest had a second negative, a slightly smaller one, made from the first by one of his colleagues at St. Mary's College. This is the one that was handed over to the bishop to give the nuns. The other one, the original, remained in his possession.

Now, let us see the explanations given by Pauline when she was (in 1926) Prioress of the Carmel of Lisieux. "This priest," she wrote, "took two photographs: one long since made public, with the mantle; the other on the other side of the Cross without the mantle. The light too harsh (*trop brutal*) on that side, made the novice uncomfortable and in consequence of it altered her features. The community therefore accepted the first negative and refused the other, as it was defective.

"We believed it had been destroyed when, after the death

THE PHOTOGRAPHS

of Blessed Teresa, the unfaithful photograph was distributed on all sides. The original negative, having been restored (*restitué*) to Carmel, Sister Geneviève (Céline), by touching up an enlargement, re-established the truth, so that one seems to see in it the servant of God at the age of sixteen" etc.

By a comparison between the original and the fake the reader is able to see that except for the face and correction to the veil the two photos come from the same negative. The "brutal light" of January—no sunshine or shadows appear in either picture—does not seem to make the novice uncomfortable. It could not have transformed an oval face into a round one. The statement that the original negative was "restituted" to the community is not clear. Who made the "restitution"? There can be no talk of restitution, where there has been no theft, and in fact Canon Gombault did not give them the original negative. We have been told that it *disappeared* after his death.

Here is another explanation which Père Noché, S.J., offers to us. He says he received it from Sister Geneviève (Céline) in August 1949.[2]

"The photograph [taken by Abbé Gombault] is bad, first, because it was taken from too low a level; secondly it thickens at 100 per cent (*épaissit à 100 per cent*) the extremely fine features of the original." [*Is Père Noché referring to Teresa herself or to a photograph? And what does this mean? We have only been able to translate this expression literally.*] Again "the original itself belongs to that kind of photo that does not reproduce the expression of the face." 'What a horrible photo' they said at the Monastery when they saw it; they returned it to the photographer. This was in 1889. . . . Much later on when the photo was distributed on all sides by Abbé Gombault, Sister Geneviève undertook to touch up an enlargement of it and the resulting portrait has the merit, in contemporary opinion, of reconstituting the expression of the face of the saint. . . ."

Thus we have now before us two sets of evidence, both

[2] C, p. 391, footnote 6.

produced by the convent. They do not agree together, nor does either of them agree with the one we have put forward.

In Père Noché's account, the brutal light of a sunless January day is not mentioned, and totally new excuses are put forward. Céline does not speak at all of two photographs or two negatives, but of one only which was returned to Abbé Gombault. Nothing is said about the "restitution" of an "unfaithful" negative to the convent. To the assertion that the merit of the fake is "to reconstitute the expressions of the saint's face", we might reply that in our opinion this new doll-like face, fabricated by Céline, has no expression whatsoever.

Both photographs, that of Canon Gombault and that supplied by the convent, are identical in many particulars. Both of them show us a young novice standing by the Cross in the centre of the quadrangle formed by the cloister. Her right arm is clumsily encircling its shaft. The crucifix of the rosary hanging from her waist rests on the plinth of the Cross. In both photos it rests there at the same place, at the same angle. The right hand and the right arm of the novice are exactly in the same position in both pictures. It is evident that both prints originate from the same negative. Both pictures profess to represent Teresa when she was sixteen and a novice, and yet both of them offer to our puzzled eyes totally dissimilar features. One face is oval, the other round. The new starched veil which the little novice had carelessly—perhaps in a hurry—fixed over her head, is in the synthetic photograph carefully and neatly arranged, and so is the top of the dress. But there can be no doubt that one and the same negative has been used for both pictures. The untouched Gombault print puts before us a face that is strong rather than pretty, humorous rather than dreamy. It is not the chocolate-box type of beauty but it possesses something better than prettiness: personality. The synthetic product on the other hand is characterless, and one could put any name under it, even that of St. Teresa, for it has no distinctive features. We have been told that, after the death of Canon Gombault, the "unfaithful" negative *disappeared*. The pamphlet we have already quoted says it was *restored* to Carmel. Since this expression generally implies some kind of dishonesty, we must protest against it. As regards the two convent accounts, it is not our business to try and reconcile the irreconcilable.

While writing this we have on our table in front of us two other pictures of St. Teresa. They were taken on June 7th, 1897, less than four months before her death. She had left her sick bed to be photographed by her sister Céline and was given a picture of the Holy Face to hold. On that day she had a very high temperature and was so weak that the gardener who was working near by, and was also the sacristan of the convent chapel, heard her exclaiming: " Oh, do hurry up, I feel exhausted."

This is well borne out by her appearance in the picture possessed by me. She looks desperately ill: puffed face, sagging cheeks, dark shadows under the eyes, deep folds at the corners of the mouth. The other photo (opposite the title page in the 1953 French edition of *Histoire d'une Ame*) shows no traces of illness. It is the smooth and rounded face of a healthy young woman of eighteen or twenty. The first one was given to someone connected with the convent very soon after the death of Teresa. The other is an official synthesis of a later date. There are some other versions of the photos taken on that same day and some of them show discreetly some little indications of illness. They have all been worked upon as if it was unbecoming or even indelicate for a saint to be ill. We know that three plates were exposed on that day, but cannot believe that any of these three could make St. Teresa look as well and healthy as we are intended to believe.

These two examples seem to confirm the general impression that the difference between the original photographs and their improved versions is so striking that they do not seem to refer to the same person. We do not say that the public at large does not prefer a doll-like beauty to a likeness faithful to the original, but we do say that if one of the two photos is a true resemblance, the other is not.

The Rev. C. C. Martindale, S.J., severely judged the correction and improvements executed by Céline. When he looks at this synthesis of pious features, "this pulpy egg-shaped head she has been supplied with . . . he has no words to express his disgust and sense of shame ".[3]

There is no need for us to say anything about the inexcusable plaster images found everywhere which pretend to be a likeness of the saint. The Catholic public seem to have a great liking for them, and since beauty and ugliness are "in the eye of the beholder" we shall waste no criticisms on them. The public want these statues, they are satisfied with them. Why should they not have them? They deserve them.

Let us come to our next point. Has anyone the right— with the best of intentions, of course—to alter historical documents? We hold very strongly the view that such documents are not a private concern. They must not in any way be altered, still less destroyed, to serve private or public feelings or interests; nor should they be corrected that they may fit in with theories or prejudices. This is a matter of common honesty. St. Teresa belongs to history, and a photograph is an historical document. The Convent of Lisieux, the sisters of Teresa, had no right to foist on the Catholic public a composite or synthetic portrait of the saint, any more than they would have had the right to alter or improve *The Story of a Soul* even with the pious purpose of edification. Historically speaking a revised document is not true any more than a synthetic photograph is true.

If a continued sense of humour is not out of place in heaven, St. Teresa may have smiled broadly when she found out that the good women she had lived with for nine years had decided that her real face was not presentable, and that they must improve her appearance before they introduced her to the Catholic public. And yet, who knows, she may have welcomed the prettiness they have inflicted on her, as well as the opulent velvet in which they have dressed her

---

[3] In a C.T.S. pamphlet, *What the Saints Looked Like* (pp. 11, 12), first published in *The Month*.

wax effigy. These beautified photographs are the pictorial legend of St. Teresa. In the same way as our own biography, if we wrote it ourselves, could only be a legend, a poetical rendering of our life, the only one of which we are aware, so also, if it depended on us, we would only transmit to posterity the painting or the photograph of ourselves which we carry in our mind: a mere poetical transcription of reality.

SECOND PORTRAIT

CHAPTER III

THE SECOND PORTRAIT

I. THE REALISTIC APPROACH

OUR first portrait of St. Teresa was an edifying version of her life, but are all its features corroborated by evidence? It seems to insinuate that as a child, as a girl, she was already flawless; that at home, at school, even in her inflexible insistence that she must enter Carmel at fifteen (not sixteen) she was invariably acting under divine inspiration. Is it true that as soon as she entered Carmel, she was recognized as a saint and "that a kind of majesty emanated from her"? Must we take literally every word she utters, every opinion she emits, as if her writings were Holy Writ?

Like the legends of old this first picture is all light, some of it perhaps artificial light. Might it be that this written portrait has been through the same processes of improvement as the photographs, as if the real Teresa was not good enough for us?

Canon G. Venzac of the Institut Catholique of Paris, in the very able article he contributed to the compendium of Abbé Combes, felt it useful to point out that "Teresa is not Jesus Christ, nor is her autobiography the Gospel, nor is her message a new Revelation". I shall likewise remind the reader that the autobiography, *Novissima Verba*, and the learned works of commentators, theologians, historians and other Theresians, are not divinely inspired. They are human works and, as such, amenable to the ordinary rules of criticism. For instance, the highly emotional character of the style of St. Teresa and her poetical exaggerations are a warning that in our interpretation of the text we must allow for a tendency to overstatement[1] She rationalized her feelings and her be-

[1] See Appendix II, *The Style of St. Teresa*.

haviour, as we all do, but must we always take it for granted that she got at the final motive, at the real meaning of her actions in every case? How few men—if any—are capable of it!

Even some of her simplest affirmations cannot be accepted literally; for instance when she says, "my father did not spoil me," though on her own evidence it is perfectly clear that he did. Not only was her old father incapable of disagreeing with her, but in this household, a French household in 1887-1888, Teresa, a big girl of twelve, thirteen, fourteen, did not take her share of housework. She did not even make her own bed. Her sisters did it for her, and like a little princess, Teresa did not wait upon herself. When Teresa says, "I was not spoilt," we are entitled to disagree.

One of her historians declares that her constant weeping when she was a child was due to the fear of having offended God or displeased her father. Some passages in her biography make this explanation improbable and even untenable. Teresa herself gives us an instance of the trivial reasons that caused her fits of weeping: "I had never been accustomed to wait on myself or do any housework, and Céline always arranged our room, but if by any chance I happened to make my bed, or brought her plants and cuttings, I should not have looked for thanks, since I was doing it for our Lord's sake, but if Céline did not seem surprised and grateful, I was disappointed and my tears started to flow."[2]

The edifying portraits keep silence over the nervous disabilities of Teresa, for they probably do not think it is right for a saint to be highly emotional. They do not seem to suspect that the headaches, the mental breakdown, the tearful disposition, the scruples, are, in fact, neurotic troubles. They are driven to say that her illness was mysterious, or due to too much study, or the work of the devil. They leave unexplained the "sufferings" to which Teresa is constantly referring and of which the people who lived with her were unaware.

We are afraid that we shall disagree on a few such points

[2] E, p. 84.

with some of our predecessors in the field. Let us protest, however, that our admiration for St. Teresa, based on reality, seems to us more genuine than one which rests on misunderstandings. We are even convinced that a presentation of the story, founded, as we believe it to be, on truth, should increase rather than diminish our devotion to a saint.

To proclaim, for instance, that Teresa was perfect from the start, is poor praise. It does not serve her glory to pretend that she had no human weaknesses and that her virtue was effortless, for it is praising her for the wrong reasons; nor in the end does it make for our edification, for it removes her so far from our common humanity that it seems useless for us to try and imitate her.

This little sketch of ours is therefore intended by us to praise St. Teresa, not by exaggerations and pious inventions, but by telling the truth as we find it. We have no intention of rubbing away the minutest particle of genuine gold on Teresa's mantle, but if it does happen that we scrape off some of the cheap gold paint others have added and which is in places beginning to tarnish, they must not be offended. We only want to serve the truth. So many of St. Teresa's friends have in the past, with the purest intentions, distorted her features, some with the pen, some with brush or chisel, that the saint must now be well inured to her admirers' blunders. We believe that in spite of it she will have one day for all of them the same radiant smile of welcome as she had for the old grumbler, Sister St. Peter.

II. CHILDHOOD AND CHARACTER

Marie Françoise Thérèse Martin was born at Alençon on the second day of January 1873, the last of the nine children of Louis and Zélie Martin. Her parents were respectively forty-nine and forty-two. Before marriage both of them had thought of embracing the religious life, and only desisted on being told it was not in a monastery that they would best serve God.

Louis Martin opened a watchmaker and jeweller's shop at Alençon in 1850, while Zélie Guérin, in 1853, started a lacemaking business in a small way in the same town. Père Piat, in his *History of a Family*, reports that one day, as they were both crossing one of the town bridges over the Sarthe, Zélie Guérin, seeing M. Martin coming towards her, heard distinctly a voice speaking to her: "This is the man I have prepared for you." We have already noted[3] that Zélie Guérin was subject to these auditive hallucinations. Five years earlier, she was wondering what she could do to earn a living, and that time also she had heard a voice saying, "Go and make Point d'Alençon lace." Following this advice, she went to a school for lacemaking, and, having learnt the trade, started a business that became very flourishing. Indeed, she was a very levelheaded woman with a marked capacity for business and a common sense attested by her correspondence. Her husband was less practical, of a sentimental turn of mind, gave way easily to tears, and had, it seems, some artistic inclinations. Leastways we know that his wife, with all her knowledge of lace making, relied on his judgment more than on her own for the choice of designs.

They were married in July 1859 and, at first, for nearly a year, lived as brother and sister. Then, in rapid succession, between February 1860 and January 1873, nine children were born. Four died in infancy, two boys and two girls. Their last child who, one day, was to be known as St. Teresa of the Infant Jesus, was not apparently of a very strong constitution, and her life was more than once in danger during the first fifteen months of her existence. During that time she was placed in the care of a foster-mother in the country, and it is only in the summer of 1874 that she returned home to her mother, having, it seems, recovered completely.

This was a very religious home. Their day, naturally,

---

[3] v. First Portrait. It is interesting to note that Charlotte Brontë had a similar experience, but the voice she heard was reciting a poem which she took down in writing. (*The Brontës*, p. 54, by E. M. Delafield.)

started with prayer, but the parents attended Mass daily, at 6 a.m. or earlier, received Holy Communion as often as the rigorist discipline of those days allowed them, and gave their daughters constant examples of practical charity towards people in need. Their conversation was less of the things of this world than of the service of God and of the future life. This, as appears in *The Story of a Soul*, was reflected in the conversations of the children, which ran on the same lines. In short, this was just the kind of a family where the vocation of a saint would be given every chance to grow and flourish. In fact all the five surviving girls became nuns, even Léonie, at one time the problem child of the family.

In her infancy Teresa possessed all the endearing characteristics of babies. Her mother watched her with a tender but clear-sighted love, while her father doted upon her uncritically. She was his little Queen; she could do no wrong, and he could never say no to her. This nearly gave rise to disagreement between Louis Martin and his wife, who had stricter ideas than he had on the subject of the training of children. Her little failings were those of any healthy child; little fits of temper when she did not get her own way, as with Victoire, the maid; babyish tantrums and moods, as when she pretended to be asleep and hid under the bedclothes; occasional moments of naughtiness—as when she tries to order her father about: "Come here yourself." For this childish impertinence, the old man had only his own softness to thank, for Teresa would not have dared to speak to her mother in this way. She loved a pretty dress that showed her little bare arms to advantage; and what is wrong with that! When all is said and done, these little failings, soon repressed, soon repented bitterly, were those of her age. They were not manifestations of her real character and we cannot attach any importance to them. What counted was this: that she had a very tender, abnormally tender, conscience which made her pathetically unhappy until she had been able to confess her baby sins to her mother and obtained full forgiveness. Her religious sense was at times embarrassingly logical (in a child of four, remember). Once she said, "Oh, Mother, how I wish you would die," and as her mother did not seem to welcome this wish with any particular enthusiasm and asked for explanations, she added, "It is because I want you to go to heaven, and one has to die first." Even at this tender age, her religion was the principal influence in her life and the mainspring of her actions. To those parents who think that religion is rather a sentiment than a discipline and a way of living, her ways, her ideas, will seem odd perhaps and certainly extreme. For this is what we read in *The Story of a Soul*:

Before she was four years old Teresa had "resolved never to refuse God anything". She already knew that holiness consisted in doing the will of God and perfect holiness in doing it perfectly. She knew the value and necessity of self-denial and, in imitation of her sisters, carried a string of beads to count her acts of virtue. Her mother took an amused interest in watching the little mite "continually putting her hand in her pocket and pulling a bead along the string for every little sacrifice".

In these actions we can already notice another component of her character: this astonishing will power of hers which twelve or thirteen years later will make possible that undeviating, indomitable pursuit of perfection, which continued steadily for nine years and is perhaps the most remarkable feature of her holiness. At three and four, she had already a great control over her actions. We have it from her own mouth: "I made it a practice," she writes, "never to complain when my things were taken, or I was unjustly accused. I preferred to keep silence rather than attempt an excuse."

III. TERESA'S MOTHER'S DEATH:
A NERVOUS BREAKDOWN

Teresa was not yet five years old when her mother died. The results of this for her were far-reaching, and went deeper than anybody realized at the time. And yet, while the poor husband's sobs proclaimed his grief all over the house, little Teresa went about dry-eyed, apparently untouched. "I did not speak to anyone of what filled my heart, I looked and listened in silence."

This is remarkable in a child so young, so fond of her mother and, later on, so much given to easy tears. For the time being she was stunned. The shock had been too much for her, and it left a permanent scar on her nervous system. It would have been better for her had she been able to give an unrestrained expression to her grief. She notes in her autobiography that from that day onwards she was a changed child. Up to then she had been happy, lively and demonstrative, now she became timid, retiring and so sensitive "that a look," she says, "was enough to make me burst into tears." Was Mrs. Martin's death the cause of this nervousness that never left her altogether, even after she had become a Carmelite, or was it only the occasion that released a weakness already part of her constitution? At this distance we cannot decide the point.

When the nurse announced to them the sad event, "Poor little things, you have no longer a mother," Teresa, hiding her head on Pauline's breast, announced: "Pauline will be my mother." Pauline was only sixteen. She was very fond of her sister and took her responsibility seriously. Her orders were obeyed both by Teresa and her father. If, for instance, M. Martin wanted to take his little Queen for a walk, it was Pauline who gave the final decision, which was not questioned by anybody.

Much as little Teresa loved her sister, much as she relied on her for everything, she found in Pauline only an inexperienced substitute. Pauline's care and solicitude had little or no effect on the new morbid sensitiveness, the timidity, the brooding that had changed the child's character suddenly after her mother's death. Anyway, she never realized how necessary she was to her little sister's well-being and at twenty decided to leave her home and to become a Carmelite nun. She had not announced it yet to the family when Teresa overheard her speaking to Marie about it. This was as hard a blow as the one she had suffered five years earlier when her mother had died. Her little world was again shattered to pieces. If Pauline went she would have no mother now, no one to confide in, no one with the authority of which she felt the need to counterbalance her own too absolute will. No wonder her little heart was broken, and this time her anguish, her bitter tears, her talk of "a trial which appeared to be far in excess of her strength" were very justified. "Pauline is lost to me," she cried. She may speak again of "wonderful peace" but she was heading for a nervous breakdown.

She herself gives us a very good account of it, and without realizing it, wrote down for us all the points of the clinical picture.[4] Pauline enters the convent on October 2nd, 1882, *A few weeks later*—Teresa was then very nearly ten years old—she begins to suffer from constant headaches. One evening her uncle, alone with her, speaks very touchingly of her Mamma. She is deeply moved and *a few hours afterwards* "her headache became extremely acute and she was seized with a strange shivering that lasted all night". Yet, when Pauline's clothing day comes, she is able to attend the ceremony, feels quite well and when she gets home and is put to bed "*she feels no trace of fatigue*". The illness returns next day. Soon she was suffering from hallucinations. She would see a precipice at the side of her bed. Nails on the wall became huge black fingers; her father's hat would assume frightening shapes. She had fits of catalepsy; she would knock her head against the bedstead or fall out on to the hard paving of her room (*without, however, hurting herself*). At last she was under the delusion that the medicaments they gave her were poisonous. "They want to poison me," she cried. Throughout her illness, Marie, her eldest sister, nursed her as a mother would have done and rarely left her side. One day she was in the garden when Teresa, from her bed, called her repeatedly and distinctly. She saw her enter the room but *failed to recognize her*. Marie holds out her arms, smiles,

[4] See the account given by Père Petitot, O.P., pp. 105-7.

calls to her, all in vain. The child does not know who she is. The reason for this is not at all obscure. It is her mother whom Teresa wanted. *Marie is not her mother, and to make it clear that she is not accepted as such, Teresa becomes incapable of recognizing her.*[5] This alone would make us certain of the nervous nature of her trouble, even if we did not possess all the other signs we have underlined. The manner in which her disorder was cured is no less conclusive. While the sisters, round her bed and much distressed, were offering prayers for the recovery of the little patient, the statue of the Virgin, facing the bed, seemed to become animated and beautiful. This was observed by Teresa alone and was not seen by her sisters. Then a sweet and compassionate smile on its face convinced Teresa that she is no longer unloved, lonely and unprotected. Now she has a mother, she is sure of it, a mother in heaven who will love and guide her. Her nervous trouble had no longer any object, filled no purpose and therefore disappeared at once.

What Doctor Notta, her physician, with his drugs and his hydropathic treatment had not done, and could not do, was suddenly and completely effected by this heavenly vision.

This sudden cessation of her nervous illness was a direct answer to the faith of the child and the prayers of her sisters. It was the work of God who planned our bodies and our minds as well as the laws that govern their mutual reactions. Should we look upon it, technically, as a miracle, that is, a suspension and a reversal of the laws of nature? We cannot think so. At Lourdes they do not consider the cure of a nervous trouble to be a miracle, and reserve this appellation to organic disorders. The illness of Teresa was due to a mental disturbance and followed a not unusual pattern. The religious mind of the child created the heavenly picture which alone could bring her comfort and recovery. If we ascribe any objective existence to the transfiguration and the smiling

---

[5] Who has not heard of the soldier who suffered from similar psychological blindness on his return home after the war of 1939-45 because he did not want to see his wife?

countenance of the statue, we can hardly refuse it to the frightening delusions which had previously visited Teresa in the course of her illness. As the latter expressed her feelings of danger and lack of protection, so the sight of a heavenly mother, powerful, smiling, loving, brought about Teresa's return to health.

After her recovery, she was in need of rest for a few days, as was only to be expected after so many weeks in bed, and the following month, in consequence of some little disagreement, she collapsed twice and lay with her limbs rigid for a few minutes. Never again did she experience such a nervous breakdown as the one she had gone through.

These various happenings, the illness—which for some months made her the most important member of the household—the vision and the "miracle" which concluded them, could not fail to leave on Teresa a deep and lasting impression, and influence her character, her conduct and perhaps her spiritual development. Now that she had been singled out by a miracle and a vision, she may have been convinced she was already a saint and possessed all the knowledge peculiar to saints. On the other hand, she may have found in these gifts only food for gratitude towards God and a new spur in her pursuit of perfection. Again, these contrary impulses may have combined together, with very odd results.

The reading of Teresa's motives of conduct during the next few years is further complicated by an unexpected sequel to the vision, which provided a good antidote against any temptations of pride. Teresa may or may not have intended to keep the secret of her vision to herself, but how could she have resisted the obstinate questioning of her eldest sister, Marie, who had so devotedly looked after her during the long illness? We cannot be surprised that Marie spoke about it to the nuns of Carmel, nor that when the child visited the convent she was plied with questions, cross-examined and made to feel that her vision was not taken seriously. Teresa imagined that perhaps, after all, she had been guilty of an untruth, and was profoundly humiliated. "My God," she wrote fourteen years later, "Thou alone knowest all I suffered." This indicates how much her pride had been wounded, how much she felt the hurt. She was still far removed from perfect humility and it was only in retrospect that she was able to write that "vanity might have crept into my heart, whereas now I was humbled".

Must we accept the theory advanced by Dr. Hans M. von Balthasar, S.J., in his *Thérèse de Lisieux*, that both her vision and the scepticism of the Sisters combined to cast "a shadow" on her spiritual development, "destroyed her sense of sin", turned her into a little actress "who had thereafter to play the saint and turn her life into a proof that her vision was genuine"?

We must agree with him that the behaviour of Teresa during the five years which followed was often peculiar, but we fail to see in it a mere reaction to the scepticism of the Sisters, any more than we can attribute to some unguarded and injudicious praise on the part of Père Pichon, S.J., her loss of a sense of sin. That it had some influence on her is probable. To what extent, we cannot tell.

It is true that this child of ten, twelve, fourteen, acts not infrequently as if she thought herself under a divine inspiration which placed her above ordinary rules. At school her companions notice that, during Mass, she will not use her Missal as everyone else does, and if an elder girl expresses disapproval, Teresa opens her book for a minute, and then shuts it again. She expects to be given signs. In confession she has no use for advice—or direction—for "she does not feel the need of any guide but Jesus". Later on we shall have occasion to observe how she expresses her disappointment by floods of tears each time she is given some advice she does not like by the Superior, by her uncle, her sister Marie, the bishop, the Vicar General, and even by the Pope. She disagrees with them all because she alone knows the will of God, while the others are blind to it. At thirteen or fourteen she is already convinced that "she already possessed such a knowledge of perfection that it could not be increased". There is also the remarkable letter she wrote to the bishop at fourteen, in which she informs him that it is through him that Jesus will fulfil His promise to her that she will enter Carmel at Christmas.

So far we must agree with Dr. von Balthasar that there are "shadows" on the sanctity of Teresa. We do not, however, attribute to her vision and to the humiliation that followed the overwhelming influence that he does. The autobiography does not say she had been forbidden to disclose her secret to Marie. If it is true that her mother had had twice the same experience as herself and had seen that same statue appear endowed with life[5a] to bring her light and consolation, Teresa must have known it and could not attribute to her own vision an exceptional or exclusive character. The event merely followed an already established pattern, in fact a family pattern.

Twice Teresa herself tells us that the humiliation she suffered at the hands of the Sisters made her look upon herself with profound contempt. It does not follow that an unworthy wish to prove herself right and the Sisters wrong turned her into a little actress, at least consciously, for all the time she was truly convinced that she was always doing God's will in all things. We should not forget, however, that she had always had a great opinion of her own importance, a feeling that had been, if anything, increased during her long illness when she saw all the routine of the household upset for her and revolving round her. Above all we must take into account the nervous weakness of Teresa, for it gives us the key of much that is otherwise inexplicable in her behaviour, of the "shadows" we have observed and of the lines her spiritual development followed.

We find the evident signs of a nervy disposition very soon after her mother's death. "With Mamma's death began the second period of my life, *the most sorrowful of all* . . ." "my

[5a] This is what a footnote (signed Carmel) states explicitly in Mgr. Thos. Taylor's translation of *The Story of a Soul*. It is not found in the latest French edition (1953). No explanation of its disappearance is given.

naturally happy disposition deserted me . . . a look was sufficient to make me burst into tears . . . I could not bear to meet strangers. . . ." She liked solitude, and at the age of six, seven, eight, would retire by herself " *to think of eternity* ". She is " an exile "; she " longs for the repose of heaven". At the age of six this is less a sign of religious fervour than one of a morbid tendency to melancholy. When we read of the constantly recurring black moods of her later years, of her scruples, of her doubts, we are confirmed in this opinion. In her childhood, she seems to have enjoyed those moods—as was the fashion among the nineteenth-century Romantics, and she even invented the word " *mélancoliser* " to describe them. As we have already observed, her nervous breakdown was not the starting point of this condition but its manifestation in an acute form.

Once we take into account this fact that Teresa was a neuropath as well as a saint, many otherwise inexplicable episodes of her life can be linked together and make a coherent whole.

It explains her constant unconscious preoccupation with herself. Neuropaths have an intense interior life, and because their sensations, their perceptions, are unusually keen, they have artistic gifts. They are dreamers. As they are much given to self-analysis, they attach an enormous importance to themselves, to what they feel, to what they do. Once, during her last illness, Pauline found her sister reading her own biography and weeping. " Why do you weep? " she said. Teresa answered, "What I read there is *so much myself*. These papers will do much good and help people to know the sweetness of God," and she added *in an inspired tone of voice*, " Oh, I know it, *everybody will love me*." She was a saint but she could not escape from herself entirely, nor from her temperament.

The impulses that come from the depths of our subconscious are all the more powerful since their source is unknown to us. Their strength often leads religious people to mistake them for the voice of God. A favourite saying of Teresa was that God does not send us impossible desires, but is God always the sender of those desires, or are we? She had desired—and how strongly—to enter the convent at Christmas, but she did not. Some months before her death she was convinced it was the will of God that she could to the end continue to work and pray with the community, but she did not. It was not the will of God.

At this stage we are not going to develop our theme any further. The evidence that we shall put forward throughout this book will reinforce our contention that the nervous disability of Teresa was the real "shadow" which she had to live and fight with to the very end, for saints cannot any more than ourselves claim exemption from bodily or mental weaknesses. The promise made to St. Paul "My grace is sufficient for thee; power is made perfect in infirmity"[5b] applied also to her and she was to remain all her life very highly strung.

Her present breakdown was cured completely, but two years later she still had headaches nearly every day and was suffering from scruples. Essentially her temperament remained what it was, although her complete surrender to God's will kept it under control, but we still find her abnormally sensitive up to the age of fourteen and highly strung to the end of her life.

One of the manifestations of this temperament was an exaggerated tenderness of conscience. She was just over twelve when, before her second Communion in 1885, she began to be tormented by scruples, and this went on for at least two years and probably much longer.[6] Such trouble is not the result of being religious or conscientious. It is a real mental disturbance that prevents one from seeing in their right proportion the elements of the little moral problems one has to solve every day. Scruples bear generally on some trifles, one or two points at a time and no more. Sometimes the patient is lax in other directions, even astonishingly so. He generally goes from confessor to confessor and finds comfort with none. As scruples have no reasonable foundation,

---

[5b] II Cor. xii, 9.   [6] E, p. 80.

they are not amenable to reason. Arguments such as Marie used with her sister who had chosen her as her confidante and director of conscience, were ineffective. Unquestioned obedience to one's confessor usually leads the way back to common sense. As Teresa herself explained it: "Every thought, every action, even the simplest, had become a source of trouble and anguish . . . one must have passed through such a martyrdom to be able to understand it." Senseless as scruples are, they are very real and very painful to the sufferer.

Teresa does not say what was the particular subject of her scruples, but it was certainly some absurd trifle, for if scruples had a reasonable cause they would no longer be scruples.

The second sign of a weakness of her nervous system was her propensity to tears. Since her mother's death she had always cried easily; this tendency was, if anything, intensified as she grew up. When she hears that her sister Marie was joining Pauline at the Carmel of Lisieux (1886), "I resolved to take no further interest here below and I shed abundant tears." "Tears at that time," she continues, "were nothing unusual, they flowed for the most trivial cause." Often she wept without any reason: "I would cry for having cried."[7] She also says that this made her almost unbearable at home. The reader must, however, try to reconcile this with the statement of an old servant—for the Roman tribunal—that she was "a very merry and very expansive child, except when she cried". She had black moods without any apparent cause: "The morrow [of her First Communion] seemed veiled in melancholy."

At school, where she was sent when she was about nine, she was a quiet child who disliked games and stood apart from the other girls. She preferred reading or thinking. "During recreation I frequently gave myself up to serious thoughts while from a distance I watched my companions at play: in fact this was my favourite occupation. Another one, which gave me real pleasure, was to pick up the little dead birds that had fallen from the trees and bury them. . . ." At

[7] E, pp. 83, 84.

home during the holidays she often hid herself in a corner of her room behind the bed curtains and there "I thought about God, the brevity of life, and eternity". This is not normal in a healthy child. The other boarders must have looked upon her as a peculiar girl, and they seem to have had little use for her. We may suggest tentatively that in spite of the kindness of the nuns towards her—she gives us examples of it—her affectionate nature did not find sufficient response. It looks almost as if at that time she was again on the brink of a serious and perhaps permanent breakdown. She says herself that these scruples made her so ill that she had to be taken from school when she was thirteen.[8] Mgr. G. Martin dismisses all these signs of a nervous temperament with a passing remark about "this truly excessive sensitiveness which from four to fourteen made Teresa so impressionable. . . ."[9] In an article professing to be a psychological study of the saint, this is really more than inadequate, more than superficial.

We must make the same reserves about his explanation of her *conversion* on Christmas night, 1886, when she was reaching her fourteenth year. Mgr. G. Martin explains it by repeating the words of St. Teresa: "Jesus transformed me." No doubt. This is true, for God looks after His own and sees to it that everything turns to their final advantage. It is true in a general way like the statements: God made me, or, God made the trees and the fruits, but it does not exclude the parents or the gardener's share in the process, and we are entitled to inquire into the secondary agents and causes that, under Providence, bring about these results. This Christmas "conversion" put an end to her distressing inclination to burst into tears on all occasions. We shall not repeat here the story of that Christmas night when it took place.[10] Enough to say that when the words of Céline brought before her eyes the picture of a grown-up girl (who incidentally intended to be a nun in twelve months' time) looking at her little Christmas presents and bursting into tears in front of

[8] E, p. 81.   [9] C, p. 192.   [10] See chapter I, pp. 12, 13.

the family, she came to her senses. She saw herself as she was, already a woman, and crying like a baby because next year there would be no Father Christmas. This ludicrous picture was too much for her sense of humour, a side of her character that developed later on at the convent. Let us add that she realized also that the source of this tearful disposition was self-pity—we might almost say selfishness. She was self-indulgent and enjoyed her emotions. "Love and a spirit of *self-forgetfulness* henceforth took possession of my heart," she says, and with the help of God's grace, "from that time her tears flowed less easily and less often." We do not add, as she does, that the fountain was dried up. In the course of the following year, we shall see that she still wept fairly easily when the decisions of the family and of the ecclesiastical authorities did not coincide with her wishes. She still had moods of excessive depression, but there was some progress and she had won her first battle and it was followed by many more victories. In Carmel, she still wept on occasions, sometimes to the surprise of the novices, but never again for a selfish reason.

M. van der Meersch offers another explanation. He suggests that a single act of will was the all-sufficient cause of her transformation. We agree that the courage must be there, but it is not enough: first, the mind must be enlightened and convinced, for common sense as much as courage is the beginning of the cure of all neurotic troubles.

She knew this, and it is the very treatment she applied to some of her companions in Carmel who suffered from that same complaint. To one who was inclined to weep easily and spoke solemnly about offering her tears to God, she explained she was merely self-indulgent. Another one was in the habit of crying over trifles and was a great nuisance to everybody. Teresa appealed to her sense of humour and taking a mussel shell on the table gathered in it the tears of the young nun until both of them, face to face, burst suddenly into laughter.

This episode of the "Christmas conversion" fifteen months before Teresa entered Carmel is important. It marks a new departure in her life, her first victory over her "nerves". We shall see later on that it was followed in the course of years by further conquests. Her tormenting doubts during the last eighteen months of her life were the last vestiges of this weakness and if they caused her much suffering, they added also much to her merits, for she never gave way to them.

IV. INNATE TENDENCIES: PRIDE AND WILFULNESS. THE JOURNEY TO ROME

To the humorous and timely warning of Canon Venzac to extremists that St. Teresa was not Jesus Christ, nor her autobiography the Gospel, one might add a further caution; she was not the Immaculate Conception and like us all she had her share of original sin. Since some hagiographers seem to invite us to believe that from the start she was perfect at all times and in all things we are obliged to enter here into explanations.[11]

We have already alluded to Teresa's pride and wilfulness: these traits were part of her character and she was apparently not always aware of them.

In the dim recesses of the unconscious lurk in us all some innate inclinations, unreasoned instincts. Allotted to each one in uneven proportions, they are the basic elements of our characters. Some of them are called bad, not because they are so in themselves, but because they are so powerful that we easily lose control of them. They seem to have their roots in a life force, the will to exist and to exist in the fullest possible manner. They are the driving power behind all human activities, and lacking it we should lead the inert life of the sloth on his tree. Without ambition, who would take on his shoulders the burdens of government? Would trade or industry flourish if no one cared for money? Should we trouble to cook and to eat, if we took no pleasure in our food?

[11] In the translation of Mgr. Thomas Taylor the French expression *amour-propre*, which means vanity, conceit or self-esteem, is generally rendered by self-love. I should like to suggest that vanity or self-esteem is more correct.

Would a bare sense of duty be strong enough to induce men to raise a family?

These blind energies, like other sources of energy, steam, electricity, atomic power, are not immoral, but they are dangerous. Keep them under control and they are a blessing. Lose command of them, let them run amok, and they become instruments of destruction, our own, and our neighbour's!

We are not disparaging St. Teresa when we assert that she was naturally proud, self-willed and obstinate. It only means that she was a daughter of Adam, and that, because she was a saint, she fought and conquered these inclinations.

As a baby she already showed some pride—commendably, on one occasion—when she refused the coin offered to her by her mother on condition that she kissed the ground. Teresa confesses that pride had some share in helping her to keep her resolutions and not to do again what she had been forbidden. She had a lively notion of her own importance, fostered unwittingly by her father, who called her "his little Queen", a title she quoted willingly and, it seems, with some complacency. "When evening came, the little Queen walked hand in hand with papa." She thought she had discovered that some stars of the constellation Orion formed the letter "T" for Teresa: her name was written in heaven! She asserts gravely that all through life nature reflects her feelings; when she weeps, it rains, when she rejoices, the sun comes out.[12] Can we be reasonably expected to believe that it rained in Rome or in Bayeux to fit in with the moods of young Teresa? What happened was that her highly sensitive temperament made her abnormally responsive to light and darkness, and the curious coincidences she noted have to be interpreted in their reverse order: cloudy, sunless weather depressed her and inclined her to moods and tears, and a bright day to well-being and optimism.

At the age of thirteen or fourteen she had a definite impres-

[12] E, p. 96. The care and detail with which ten years later she records these moods shows the importance she attached to them and the enjoyment she found in feeling her feelings.

sion that she had nothing more to learn about perfection, and what she said on this subject could, we think, find place here, under the heading of unconscious pride: "I often wondered what greater knowledge of perfection could come to me later on, for I thought it impossible to acquire a better understanding of it than I had then."[13]

Of this period of her life, she says: "If scholars who had spent all their life in study had come to question me, they would, I am certain, have been astonished to see that a fourteen-year-old child understood the secret of perfection—a secret which all their learning could not discover, for to know it one must be humble of spirit."[14]

Yet already, as a child, she turned to spiritual profit this great notion she had of her importance. At eleven, at the time of her First Communion, she decided to aim high and felt she had it in her to succeed. "I was born for great things and it was made known to me that my personal glory would consist in becoming a saint." And "I feel the same daring confidence that I shall become a *great saint*". This is an uncommon and praiseworthy purpose, but, expressed in these words, "my personal glory", "a great saint", it leaves one wondering. Which of us at eleven would have dared plan his life on these ambitious lines! That Teresa should, at eleven, feel like this and be in no doubt that she would succeed, manifests great faith and trust in God, but it shows she was aware she could rely also on the unswerving power of her young will. Mother Marie de Gonzague, the Prioress of the Lisieux Carmel, with all her failings, did not lack insight, and this may have been what she had in mind when she was heaping humiliations on the child and declaring to her sister Pauline that "her pride is much greater than you think: she must be humbled constantly". She need not have been afraid of the results. Teresa knew how to press even her pride into the service of her spiritual formation.

We now come to a feature of St. Teresa's character which

[13] E, p. 132.
[14] Quoted by Mr. John Beevers in his *Storm of Glory*, p. 55.

is most conspicuous in her autobiography: her tremendous will power. M. van der Meersch sums up the child as being wilful and obstinate to a prodigious degree. This is strongly contested by his critics, who are not, however, very forthcoming in offering an alternative version of their own. They seem afraid of exaggerating the importance of her will in her obstinate pursuit of holiness, and in so doing of minimizing the share of God's grace in it. One of them agrees that she had a strong will, another speaks of her as a "docile little saint". Another quotes one of her sayings: "I have never done my will on earth."[15] Let us not forget that one can be at the same time very wilful and very obedient without contradiction, for obedience may demand as great an exertion of will as rebellion. It seems evident to us that it is the outstanding single-mindedness and will power with which Teresa had been endowed that made possible her uninterrupted pursuit of perfect obedience and other virtues.

She did not reach perfection all at once, and we must not be misled by her assurance that "she had never done her own will". That she was convinced of it goes without saying, for she was completely sincere, but, like many self-willed people, when she wanted something badly and had made up her mind, she managed always to persuade herself that it was also the will of God. This is not particularly uncommon among superiors, and we ourselves have been informed sometimes by wilful people that they were obeying God's will, when they were only having their own way. Let us add that they seem always unconscious of any subterfuge. On some occasions it looks very much as if Teresa was not immune from these little pieces of self-deception. Once, she had been praying for a celebrated murderer, Pranzini, and was anxious for a sign that her prayers had been answered. "Papa," she confesses, "never allowed us to read newspapers." Yet, on the morning after his execution, she did not hesitate, and hastily opened the paper to see whether he had shown signs of repentance on the scaffold. Why does she say: "I did not consider it an

[15] C, p. 80.

act of disobedience"? What was there to stop her asking for permission first? Did she argue with herself that her father would have no right to object, or that anyway he never found fault with anything she did, or was she afraid that he might say no? At the Coliseum their poor old father "called loudly" to Teresa and Céline not to go down into the arena. They did not listen to him. Why? "Only one thought filled my mind," she says, "I must reach the arena." When they returned "Papa had not the heart to scold us". Everywhere during this journey to Rome, in Loreto as in the Catacombs, she could never take no for an answer. A docile little saint!

If we have any doubts left about this young girl being, as the novelist puts it, "wilful and obstinate to a prodigious degree", we need only observe the inflexible tenacity that took her to Bayeux and to Rome in pursuit of the fulfilment of her plans. She had made up her mind that she must enter Carmel as a postulant before Christmas 1887, that is, before the completion of her fifteenth year, instead of waiting at least until she reached the age of sixteen. In such a home as hers, her vocation was not in danger and there appeared to be no special reason why this exceptional step should be taken, though one can see quite a few why it should not. Young ladies of fifteen are apt to change their minds as they grow up. A child of that age could not be expected to keep the austere rules of Carmel without some danger to her health; or, if she did not, it might be an example that would introduce a spirit of laxity among the Sisters. Her old father earlier in the year had already had his first stroke and had not quite recovered. Teresa herself noticed during the journey to Rome that he was often exhausted and in pain. And finally there was opposition on the part of the superiors on whom the decision rested. Let us point out that it is usual and reasonable, as a rule, to accept as the expression of God's will the repeated and clear decisions of our superiors. But all the time she had a no less clear conviction that she alone knew what the will of God was.

Among those who opposed her desires we cannot include

her father, for he could be relied upon at all times to agree with whatever his little Queen would decide. But if we cannot include her confessor, it is for a totally different reason. We can take it that he was never consulted. For it is worth noting that, just before she begins the tale of the obstacles she met to her vocation, she refers to him in these terms: "In those days I did not speak of my intimate feelings to my confessor, for the road I trod was so direct, so clear that I did not feel the need of any other guide but Jesus." This was what she thought. But we have it from her that while she was suffering from scruples she went to her sister Marie for direction. She speaks of her wonderful teaching, of the torrents of eloquence that gushed from her lips. "I told everything to Marie, I laid open before her all my thoughts, even the most extravagant. . . . This done, I experienced a momentary peace. . . ." It seems probable that a good confessor would have known better than Marie what was needed: a firm hand, and less sympathy, clear orders, and less reasoning. It is relevant at this point that when "dearest Marie, the support of my soul"[16] disagreed with her on this subject of entering Carmel at fifteen, Teresa found her visits to her at the convent more and more distressing. She had expected approval, and instead she was being given advice. A confessor might perhaps have agreed with Marie, and how would Teresa have dealt with him?

They had all disapproved: Mother Prioress had said that sixteen was the earliest age when she could be admitted; the ecclesiastical superior, Canon Delatroëtte, said bluntly: not before twenty-one; a very sound decision, since it was not apparent to him that Teresa's case would prove exceptional. Her uncle, at first, was uncompromisingly of the same opinion. See what happens. After her visits to Marie, great distress, after her interview with the Canon, "her soul is overcast with heavy clouds". When she leaves her uncle, her soul is overwhelmed with grief; all round was night, dark night, utter desolation, death! Yet nothing can stop her. She goes to the

[16] E, pp. 80, 93.

bishop, who does not take her seriously, and finally to the Pope. The final scene at the Vatican is illuminating.

The group of pilgrims to which she belonged attended the Pope's Mass in his own private chapel and later on were received in audience by him. According to custom, every pilgrim went up in turn to the dais where the Pope was seated. They knelt, received his blessing and then retired to the adjoining hall. The director of the pilgrimage and Vicar General of Bayeux, who was standing at the right of Pope Leo XIII, " announced in a loud voice that he absolutely forbade anyone to address the Holy Father ". Teresa's heart beat wildly but Céline whispers: "Speak." The next moment, on her knees before the Pope, she formulates her request. Surprised and displeased, the Vicar General explains the situation, and the Pope, as could be expected, says, " Well, my child, do whatever the superiors may decide." She cannot accept that and insists. The Pope again, instead of granting the request, merely replies, " Well, child, you will enter if it be God's will." Her hands were still resting on the knees of His Holiness, she was going to continue pleading, when the Noble Guards came, took her by the arm, lifted her to her feet and led her away, weeping, to the next room.[17]

To us, this unseemly insistence, and the " crushing sorrow " that follows the kindly and reasonable words of the Pope, merely show that Teresa had still a long way to go to reach the perfect spirit of acceptance that we observe in her a year later at the convent. A day came when she confessed: " When I think over my novitiate days I see clearly now how far removed I was from perfection; some things there are that make me laugh." She might, with more reason still, have applied these words to herself as she was two and three years earlier.

Meanwhile, the assurance of the Pope that the will of God will eventually be done did not seem to console her at all. In fact, " my sorrow is crushing . . . and the Italian sky, now veiled with heavy clouds, mingled its tears unceasingly with

[17] E, pp. 113, 114.

mine. . . . All was over." Again she tells us of the peace that dwelt in the depths of her heart. Writing this ten years after the events, she may have spoken more of what she hoped she had felt, than of what she did feel at the time.

Her obstinacy and her tears can only be explained by the conviction that not only was she right, but that she was seeking the will of God and that her mission was to make everyone execute it.[18] She felt sure that in refusing to accept the rulings of her eldest sister, Marie, of the superior of the convent, of the bishop, and we might almost say, of the Pope, she was only trying to make the will of God triumph over the blindness of men. Eventually she entered the convent, not as she had said God willed it, at Christmas, but three months later.

Very tentatively we shall suggest a possible reason for her insistence on entering the convent at the unusual age of fifteen. There was no one at home who could withstand her, her father less than anyone. The phrase: *I insisted* and my noble father *yielded* represents fairly their respective positions. Through one of these contradictions one meets with, not infrequently, in human beings, she may have been hankering for the strong hand, the firm will, that would guide her and compel her obedience, precisely because her own will might lead her astray. This she did not find at home. Remember that, long before this, she had said, "one thing only do I fear, and that is to follow my own will". Realizing its power, she wondered where it might lead her. Was she so sure after all that her will was, and always would be, a safe guide to follow? She was afraid. She wanted her freedom to be taken from her, she wished to be under rules, under a discipline she could not question, and the convent appeared to her as a place of refuge and of safety, where, in obedience, she knew that she would without doubt find the will of God. Years afterwards she wrote: "Oh, my God, from how much disquiet do we free ourselves by the vow of obedience."[19] The whole

[18] Letter to the bishop quoted in next chapter, in the first paragraph.
[19] E, p. 160.

of that paragraph can be read as a comment on her own past wilfulness.

What perhaps gives some colour to our suggestion is the perfect obedience she showed from the first day of her arrival in Carmel until the end. Let us add that, if we realize the intensity of her will power, this humble obedience will appear all the more astonishing and meritorious.

Faced with a tenacity of purpose he had never met before, the bishop finally gave way. He thought at first he was dealing with a child; and instead he found before him a resolute woman. "Woman's will, God's will", say the French, knowing well that a determined woman always wins and that it saves time in the long run to agree promptly.

CHAPTER IV

POSTULANT AND NOVICE

1. FIRST JOYS AND DISAPPOINTMENTS

THE bishop's consent did not come all at once, for he did not give way all along the line. Teresa had said "Christmas" and, in order to convince Mgr. Hugonin of the importance of this date, had written and assured him that "Little Jesus has made it clear to me that He wanted me at Christmas". She added that "Jesus had made her the promise and that it was through the bishop He was going to fulfil it".[1] The bishop was evidently not impressed by these declarations and did not see the same urgency as Teresa did about the precise date of her entry into Carmel; it was only three days after the Nativity that he sent Mother Prioress his authorization to receive this very young lady in her convent. In her turn Mother Marie de Gonzague, feeling that the austerities of Lent were too much for a girl of fifteen, wrote to her on January 1st that the bishop's consent had come but that nevertheless she must wait until Lent was over. After so many weeks of waiting, this was a hard blow and Teresa wept. Her first reaction prompted by disappointment was a sudden longing to throw off restraint and enjoy her last three months of freedom. Resisting this impulse, and taking herself in hand, she turned the weeks of waiting into a time of preparation against the days when she must live by rule and obey instantly the summons of the bell. She mortified her headstrong inclinations by checking them again and again, and this self-imposed discipline proved of immense value for the new life that was about to begin for her.

[1] Quoted by Mr. John Beevers in *Storm of Glory*.

When the doors of Carmel closed upon her on April 9th, 1888, she left outside her father, Léonie and Céline in tears; in the convent, waiting for her, she found Pauline, whose departure six years earlier had caused her strange illness, and Marie, whose presence and guidance she had also missed acutely. After their long separation, what a welcome she must have received, and what a joy she must have felt! We may surmise also that the arrival of this young recruit caused much excitement among the Sisters and that on this great day, Teresa saw herself surrounded on all sides by kind and smiling faces.

At first the novelty and strangeness of everything was a delight. These twenty nuns who, to her, appeared all so holy and at the same time, during the recreation hour, so cheerful, were her new family. What peace dwelt here in the silence of the house, a silence made all the more impressive by a few disciplined sounds: muffled, unhurried footsteps in the passages, the jingling of a rosary, the opening or the shutting of a door somewhere in the distance. Peace of heart also. She found it in the holy silence of the chapel, in the soft echoes of women's voices reciting together the Divine Office, and, most of all, at evening in the semi-darkness when the flicker of the lamp, the live flame before the tabernacle told her of the presence of her divine Bridegroom, as she called Jesus. Peace also in her tiny cell with its rough and scanty furniture, the hard bed, the low stool and the little table; peace undisturbed by pride of possession, by wish for luxuries; for she found there neither ornaments, nor curtains, nor carpets, nor coverlets; none of those fripperies which in 1888 accumulated in the stuffy houses of the French *bourgeois* and conferred on them the seal of respectability. The little jug on the shelf, the hour-glass on the table, delightful toys as they looked to her, could not be counted as luxuries; they were necessities.

From the first Teresa loved her cell, and all the more because it was so poor.[2] In it she felt as far from the world as

[2] E, p. 122.

she would have been in the desert of her childish fancies. In it she found a solitude which was not loneliness, for on the wall, always before her eyes, was a crucifix, the token of God's love for man, a constant reminder that, watching over her, giving sweetness to her very trials, was the One she had come to meet here, that she might the better love Him in silence and solitude.

She did not know yet that, nine years later, casting a last look at the little room and leaving it for ever, she would sum up what it had meant to her and say to Pauline, her sister, "Much of my [future] happiness has been won in this cell, for I have suffered so much in it that I should be glad to die there."

The first days in Carmel had for her the charm and unreality of a honeymoon; for a while every moment brought a joy and a new delight to the little bride. Not for long. Life in the cloister is not, as the world imagines, one of leisurely dreaming and floating between heaven and earth, but one in which one has still to deal with human beings and, hardest of all, with oneself.

Almost at once she was assigned a few tasks, simple ones, such as sweeping staircases and passages, or helping Sister Marie des Anges, the Novice-Mistress, in the linen room. This Sister was a saintly woman, kindly, humble, but of a simplicity that inspired more respect for her virtue than for her intellect.[3] She had to teach the new postulant how to mend and patch, and probably little else, for Carmelite poverty compels the nuns to use their well-worn garments and their bedclothes long after people in the world would have thrown them away. Let us concede at once that in none of these tasks was Teresa very proficient. In justice to Mother

---

[3] Once a toy balloon carried by the wind landed in the courtyard of the convent and air currents moved it about bumping and bobbing in such an uncanny manner that a Sister concluded it must be a diabolical visitation. Seizing a stick, she rushed fearlessly at the devil, who under her repeated blows, burst with a groan and a hiss. Teresa witnessed the scene and greatly enjoyed it. The heroine of the battle was none other than the Mistress of Novices. (C, p. 305.)

Prioress and of some of the Sisters whom we might otherwise accuse of being unduly strict, let us admit that Teresa was as clumsy in plying her needle as in handling the broom.

* * *

The monastery, the cell, the dress, the lengthy prayers in chapel do not alone make one a saint. Teresa had still a long way to go. We have already noted a remark of hers in later years that some of her notions of perfection when she was a novice would now make her laugh. A short time before she died, a Sister asked her if she had ever had to fight against her nature. Teresa answered that she had a difficult nature and had to fight very often.

She had run away from the world at fifteen, with what alacrity we have already observed. From the first moment, almost, the contrast between expectation and reality must have called for heroism. She found in the convent not only the discipline, obedience, and austerities she had anticipated, but humiliations and spiritual trials that she had not; yet these were precisely what was needed to train and shape the saint-to-be. She had known all along that her life in Carmel must be one of sacrifice, but she had not imagined what form this would take. She knew that in a convent, a too-human or exclusive affection for one's companions cannot be allowed, but she was not prepared to meet indifference or at times hostility. She may have suspected that her nature was a wilful and proud one, she may have been aware of the great opinion she held of her own importance, but only experience could teach her how arduous would be the fight if she was to keep those imperfections down.

Above all she had embraced the religious life to feel herself nearer her Lord, but even this consolation was taken from her. "I experienced," she says, "great aridity." This she may not have foreseen. She had entered Carmel to devote herself to the contemplative life; she may have reasonably expected that, having given up all worldly pleasures and duties, she would, in the cloister, receive from her beloved Lord a new and fuller response; that, in prayer and meditation, her heart would burn within her as with the disciples at Emmaus when the Lord spoke to them; that before the altar, near the tabernacle where Jesus resides, she would feel Him present, listening, answering. She had perhaps expected to find in Carmel, the love, the raptures, the turmoil of emotions she tried to express in her poems; but God seldom discovers to us the shape of the sacrifices to come. Instead of finding consolation in her devotions, she felt nothing and had nothing to say except to offer to God this very emptiness of mind. She prayed no less, but went through her prayers without the satisfaction of love felt and returned: In 1889 her "suffering" reached its height. Her spiritual aridity increased and she found no comfort in heaven or on earth.[4] Her prayers, her Communions, lacked that sense of reality which would have made for happiness. She felt as one would, who, working and sacrificing oneself for the Beloved, received no sign that it has been noticed or appreciated; as one who would love and never hear a loving word in return.

And yet she declares that "her happiness was calm and peaceful", that "amid these waters of tribulation she was the happiest of mortals". This sounds puzzling, but she kept her faith and her feelings in separate compartments. Her Lord seemed absent and silent; hence she speaks of the waters of tribulation. She knew and believed He was near, looked on and approved, and this gave her a conviction of happiness. We have already remarked on this opposition, this duality in the mind of Teresa. What she calls happiness sounds to us somewhat bleak considering the frequency and intensity of her feelings of desolation. To her both emotions were equally real and apparently co-existed together in her consciousness.

Another unforeseen ordeal was the drastic treatment Teresa received at the hands of Mother Marie de Gonzague, whose

[4] E, p. 131.

former kindness seemed to have changed overnight into a relentless severity. "Our Lord," she says, "permitted that Mother Marie de Gonzague—sometimes unconsciously—should treat me with much severity. She never met me without finding fault and I remember on one occasion when I had left a cobweb in the cloister she said to me before the whole community: 'It is easy to see that our cloisters are swept by a child of fifteen. It is disgraceful. Go and sweep away that cobweb and be more careful in the future.' On the rare occasions when I spent an hour with her for spiritual direction, she seemed to scold me nearly all the time. . . ." Once the Prioress, meeting her on her way to the garden where she had been sent by the Mistress of Novices to do some weeding, exclaimed: "Really this child does absolutely nothing. What are we to think of a postulant who must be sent out for a walk every day. And this was the invariable method of dealing with me. . . ." Perhaps, on reading this page, we might feel some indignation at the thought of the cruelty practised by the Prioress on a defenceless child of fifteen and approve of M. van der Meersch's forceful language when he calls her a Judas and a Cain, unless we remember that Teresa is often over-emphatic and says more than she really means. We must make allowance here for exaggerations arising from a highly strung temperament. This applies particularly to her reference to the five years of misery which followed when Mother de Gonzague was Prioress: "Unknown to anyone this was the path [of suffering] I trod for fully five years." Further on, alluding to her own deliberate avoidance of her sisters, she said "I could not see you" and "Oh, my little mother, how much I suffered then. . . . I could not open my heart to you and I thought you did not know me any more". No one can contest that this was an exaggeration, for Teresa could have obtained the permission to speak to her sisters, to open her heart to Pauline as often as she needed by the simple process of asking for it.[5]

What is clear is that, at the time, the scoldings and humilia-

[5] C, p. 367.

tions she went through were bitterly felt by Teresa, and that nine years later she could not remember them calmly. The passage of time had not blotted out the pain they had caused her. "Invariable treatment"—"unknown to anyone"—she says. Surely a heavy cross for a child of fifteen, and no one but Teresa could have borne it. Yet, this was probably the heroic treatment she needed. The Prioress explained to Pauline: " You wish me to put Sister Teresa forward: it is the reverse that should be done. She is much prouder than you think; what she needs is to be constantly kept down."[6] On consideration it seems to us that the reprimands were not always undeserved nor excessive, and would not have hurt a young woman less acutely sensitive than Teresa was. She had entered Carmel to be tested and trained in many ways. Her vocation was one of mortification and penance and she says that from the first "she took suffering fondly to her heart". More than once afterwards she recognized that the Prioress had acted rightly, and she thanks her for not having spared her.[7] She was not perfect yet and if, in the tale of her sufferings we can still hear some echo of the repressed resentments of long ago, something like the last rumbling of a storm that is over, it is merely because for a moment while she was writing, she lived all over again those days of bitter struggle. The battle was won; she remembered the wounds. Do not forget that this battle was not fought against the Prioress but against herself. All the time she was progressing with giant strides along the road of obedience, detachment, humility, silence, cheerful acceptance.

One more remark. Teresa says that what she endured was unknown to anyone. This is quite true. In a small community nothing escapes observation. They see and hear everything, and yet the Sisters never noticed any signs of undue severity. On the contrary they thought to the last she had been spared suffering and humiliation.[8] If anything, they

[6] *Summ.*, p. 308. Par. 755 quoted by A. Noché.
[7] E, pp. 150-1.
[8] N.V., p. 96, July 29th.

would have said that, at the beginning at least, she received a favoured treatment. This seems to indicate that the sensitiveness of Teresa was at the root of a good deal of what she calls her "sufferings".

II. THE PRIORESS AND HER COMMUNITY; THE TRAINING OF THE WILL

The portrait drawn by M. van der Meersch rests on a legend of diabolical hatred for Teresa on the part of the Prioress and of general dislike on the part of the nuns. This is due to an exaggerated and distorted interpretation of the facts.

The Prioress was very strict with Teresa, possibly more than was necessary. Some of the nuns also were not very fond of her, at least in the beginning. Whether the motives of Mother de Gonzague were as highly principled as she imagined must remain an open question. Whether the Sisters were often deliberately unkind to her, must be decided on probabilities. Since we must make up our mind on these points, in order to form a just appreciation of what life in the convent meant for Teresa, we shall now put before our readers, not merely our own impressions, but the facts as far as they are known to us, so that they may be able to form their own judgment.

Mother Marie de Gonzague, as head of the convent, played a very important part in the life—and some say in the death also—of Teresa. As such she deserves more than a passing mention. If the photograph facing page 245 of the 1953 French edition of *The Story of a Soul* can be taken as a guide, we should say that her face is of a decidedly masculine cast, and speaks of will power and decision. It is the face of an old woman, but a strong face, and we cannot find any traces of former good looks which might have explained the attraction some of the young nuns seem to have felt towards her. Opinions about her differ. Père A. Noché, S.J., tells us that she was "autocratic, irascible, changeable, impulsive, devoted to her family and to her cat, Mira. She did not always enforce on others the rule of silence, nor did she keep it herself." He considers her "to have possessed energy as well as business capacity. She was a woman of wise counsel. She had great lights and a lofty outlook on spiritual matters."[9] In order to obtain a balanced impression of her character let us mention a few episodes of her life in the convent. Some people would call her a neurotic. This would not preclude intellectual gifts, even of a high order, nor even attractiveness. When she was sub-prioress, she disappeared once in a fit of jealousy for a whole day, and was eventually found in a corner of the garden crouching under a ladder. Following this, she tried to commit suicide by throwing herself out of the window. Her affection for Mira, the cat, led her to break the strict rule of silence at night when pussy had gone astray, and to send the community in search of her. As a reward for catching a rat, she promised an extra Communion to one of the nuns. She encouraged among the Sisters the practice of crazy penances, such as flagellation with nettles. She intrigued and indulged in convent politics to ensure her re-election as Mother Prioress. In defiance of a recent papal decree of Leo XIII she wanted to keep to herself the right to regulate the number of Communions made by the nuns, and she intimidated the chaplain who insisted on observance of the new rules.[10]

In spite of all this, most Sisters seem to have been devoted to her, and she was elected and re-elected Prioress for many years, which only proves that in convents, as in the world outside, cold common sense is not always the privilege of the majority. We may credit her with religious sense, sincerity and good intentions and, even if she disliked Teresa at the beginning, she may have acted with good conscience according to her lights. But it remains that she acted sometimes in an irresponsible manner and possessed little control over herself. She was not fitted by temperament for the contemplative life, but for a life of action. In the world she would have

[9] C, p. 351. "Femme de tête et de bon conseil; des lumières et des vues spirituelles élevées; zèlée pour le bien."
[10] *Storm of Glory*, pp. 78-9.

been looked upon as a brilliant and even as a normal woman.

Whether her conduct towards Teresa during the first five years was inspired by spiritual solicitude or instinctive dislike must remain an open question. Her attitude during the saint's last illness is also something of an enigma. Mother de Gonzague, in the years that followed, seems to have convinced herself that she had acted with the purest intentions.[11] It seems certain that before the end she came to appreciate fully the great virtue of the saint. Both spoke of each other with affection and admiration.

For some time—and presently we shall enlarge on this—Teresa's manner and deportment were not calculated to inspire affection in her companions or her superiors. She was not quite like everyone else. She may even have struck them at first as a bit singular. She was giving everyone good example, but, as she confessed it later on, was itching to teach and reprove nuns older than herself. At sixteen she was inclined to speak her mind even to Mother Superior. In short, she was burning to put everybody right. She acted, no doubt, from the highest motives, but this procedure does not usually make one popular.

Our interpretation of the attitude of the Prioress would be —moods and tantrums apart—something like this: In a small community, the four Martin sisters, plus one of their cousins, Marie Guérin, might have formed a block of opposition that would have undermined a superior's authority. Teresa herself realized it, and, for this reason, deliberately kept her sisters at a distance. The possibility of a coalition against her haunted the Prioress, for she was ambitious and loved to have power and authority. Her fears seemed to materialize when, in 1893, in spite of an intensive campaign for votes, she failed to be re-elected and had the mortification to see one of the four Martin sisters—Pauline—take her place and become her Prioress. It was always Pauline she had feared and perhaps detested, not young Teresa, because Pauline had inherited all the business aptitudes of her mother for planning and execu-

[11] Evidence of Père Godefroy Madelaine. C, p. 363. Note.

tion, push and efficiency. If this is correct, it gives us the key to the interpretation of many incidents. It was the fear of giving too much influence to one family in the convent that prompted the Prioress to try and send two of the sisters abroad.[12] It was this that may have partly caused Teresa to remain in the novitiate until she died instead of taking her place in the Chapter; that prevented her being Mistress of the Novices instead of merely their companion. On the other hand it is Pauline who, later on, clearly lays some blame at the door of the Prioress for not allowing Dr. le Néele to visit Teresa, when it was very necessary he should, and for refusing to have hypodermic injections of morphia given to alleviate her sufferings.

Mother Marie de Gonzague was—perhaps unconsciously, as Teresa herself has suggested—the instrument of Providence. A kinder, more indulgent Prioress might well have ruined her vocation, while her indifference and her severity discouraged the sentimental display of affection which Teresa was only too ready at the beginning to indulge in. Humiliations counteracted the influence of a home where no one had ever scolded her, since everyone thought her perfect (an angel in human shape, said Pauline). Housework, as distinct from drawing-room accomplishments, taught her discipline. Under these influences we see her conquering her pride, for she is made to feel unimportant and almost useless. She learns to accept an unfair scolding without any sign of discomposure or resentment, without even an attempt at justification. In short, a treatment that would have driven out of the monastery one with a less certain vocation only confirmed Teresa in hers and led her to the summits.

On the part of the nuns there was none of the soft indulgence, of the petting, that a young girl might have expected, and the older women given, as something natural and excusable. Nor did they treat her like a little prodigy or like a little saint. We have before us the assertion of Mother Marie

[12] E, p. 159.

des Anges that from the beginning "she astonished the community by conduct marked with a kind of majesty!" We cannot attach any importance to this testimonial, contrary as it is to other evidence. The rest of the community was not so easily impressed as the simple Mistress of Novices.

In the linen room, where Teresa worked under her, there was another Sister, an expert with the needle, who showed some impatience at the slowness and clumsiness of a fellow worker who evidently had never learnt sewing at home. The mending was not done, or badly done, and the result was an accumulation of work in arrears. With the authority conferred by age and craftsmanship—and also with some resentment—the Sister did not spare the postulant outspoken advice and sharp criticism. There is no reason to believe that Teresa resented her remarks, which were, after all, justified, but we are allowed to conclude that this Sister's words sprang more from disapproval than from veneration.

Perhaps the "majesty" conferred on Teresa by Mother Marie des Anges was in reference to a mannerism of hers in which she did not persevere for long, but which at first she may have considered to be a suitable expression of inward feelings. We may remember that during her First Communion retreat at school, she had attracted attention by carrying a big crucifix in her belt. At the convent she was seen walking very solemnly and slowly, with eyes downcast, and this affectation annoyed some of the Sisters.[13] One of them spoke loudly enough to be overheard: "Look at her, the way she walks, how slow she is! She is in no hurry to start her work. She was no good at anything." This kind of criticism was just what young Teresa needed, for, being full of good sense, she benefited by it. Some years later, she saw a young novice sauntering towards the laundry and quickly overtaking her she remarked: "Is this the way people hurry when they have children at home and must work to earn money for their food?"

---

[13] Once at the seminary of V. during a retreat, the preacher gave the students this piece of sound advice: "*Messieurs, surtout ne prenez pas des airs penchés.*" (Don't try to look pious.)

There was no malice in these and kindred observations. They are the salt of life and belong to the daily give and take of any community, big or small. Teresa, being sensitive, may have felt them more acutely than others would. Years later she still remembered that people had said that " she was slow and not keen on her duties " and with reference to this period of her life, that is the beginning of her second year at the convent, she speaks feelingly of the many pin-pricks to which she was subjected (which shows that she was not popular in all quarters) and which caused her much suffering.[14] But it is not said anywhere that she wept as easily and frequently as she would have done a year or two earlier. She had mastered this weakness in so far as it was caused by selfish motives.

It may be apposite to record here that later on, as companion of novices, she never shrank from giving unpalatable warnings to her charges, at the risk of upsetting them, if she judged it necessary. Even a few weeks before her death " she corrected a novice very severely ". On August 9th she said: " No later than yesterday I used my sword [her tongue] on a novice," and on the 19th, she sharply admonished another one who had come to see her: " You must not sit that way on a chair. It is in the Rule."[15] If we pretended that nuns must only murmur sweet nothings to one another all day long it would only show either that we are insincere or that we know nothing about women or convents.

Saints, unless they have the sense of humour and the well-balanced judgment of a St. Francis of Sales, can be very irritating. Their own high standards are a silent reproach to the others, and their singularities can be a nuisance and a vexation. Long after the death of Teresa a Sister declared that she avoided her " not through lack of esteem but because I found her too perfect ". She may have expressed herself more bluntly when the saint was alive. Céline confessed that at times she found her young sister somewhat trying. One

[14] Letters, I, 97. LI, p. 100. Quoted by A. Noché, S.J. C, p. 316.
[15] N.V., pp. 40, 133, 145.

cold day, when it was freezing hard, she found Teresa spreading her bare hands on her knees. It looked like showing off her spirit of mortification, and Céline, exasperated, said so, to which Teresa gave no answer except a knowing (*malin*) little smile. Céline did not like it and, years afterwards, remembered it when evidence was being collected for the canonization. This was merely a childish lack of discretion on the part of Teresa but it shows how the very perfection of saints, if not kept tactfully in the background, can irritate those less-advanced people who have to live with them. This may explain the attitude of another nun who, consciously or not, must have disliked Teresa, since she felt impelled to contradict her and contest everything she said, on every occasion. Others, through no fault of their own, but through lack of intelligence or education, through old age or ill health, were bound to be trying. Such was Sister St. Raphael, a woman of weak intellect; Sister Marie de St. Joseph, a neurasthenic and somewhat irresponsible; or Sister J-B, whose narrow and stern piety was the symbol—Teresa said—of God's severity. Such people as these would try the patience of a saint, as the saying is, but Teresa had made penance her special vocation and she looked on these people and their company as a God-sent occasion to practise patience and charity. She saw them as sick people to be pitied and cared for, and in spite of the boredom or annoyance they inflicted on her, she remembered their past merits and their real virtues. She asked for Sister St. Joseph to be made her helper in the linen room[16] and endured her company for three years. No one else was able to follow her example and finally the Sister, a confirmed mental case, had to leave the convent.

Teresa did not see unkindness where none was intended. Once a nun, helping her to fix on her scapular, did it so clumsily that she ran a long pin into the muscles of her shoulder; a venomous token of dislike had it been deliberate, as has been suggested in some quarters! But is there the

[16] It was not the same Sister as the first fellow worker in that department.

slightest reason for us to think so, when we remember that before the invention of safety-pins, this was a daily occurrence in nurseries, when mothers, loving but careless, pinned the swaddling-clothes to the tender flesh of their babies. In the wash-house, a Sister beating the wet linen with her wooden bat, or wringing it too vigorously, splashed Teresa with dirty water; a clumsy, slovenly thing to do, but must we suppose it was intentional? Teresa was annoyed, but, after a moment of hesitation, kept down her rising temper and found in the splashing a welcome occasion of penance and patience.

There remain, however, a few incidents that may indicate some antagonism and a certain intention to hurt. It is stated in the *Summarium*[17] that one of the Sisters in the kitchen did not like Teresa. In the Epilogue of *The Story of a Soul*, it is also said that the Sisters in the kitchen, finding her easy to please, *invariably served her* with whatever was left, a desiccated omelet, may be, or an uneatable herring that had been cooked and re-cooked half a dozen times. Did this proceed from a natural tendency on the part of the cooks to follow the line of least resistance, and dispose of their mistakes in the quarter where no protest would be made, or was it a deliberate sign of dislike? Perhaps both.

In the little town where the family was well known, some ill-natured comments had been made on the mental disorder which afflicted M. Martin, and the alleged heartlessness of his daughter in leaving him to the care of strangers. They even suggested that the loss of his favourite daughter had contributed to bring on his condition. These rumours found their way into the convent through visitors and inevitably, in an assembly of women, four of whom were daughters of the sick man, the embarrassing subject must have cropped up in the conversation. Discreet allusions, charitable words of commiseration, half repressed smiles at the eccentricities of the poor man, hearty indignation at the unkind comments of the town people, nothing was spared to the four sisters. That

[17] *Summ.*, Par. 2218, quoted in a footnote of C, p. 340.

Teresa suffered very much from this tactless gossip we know well; that it was due to calculated unkindness on the part of the nuns, we have no right to insinuate, but the stupidity of a friend can hurt as much as the hatred of an enemy.

"There are no enemies in Carmel," declared Teresa. Nevertheless she found there what she called "imperfect souls", the people whom everybody shuns, and whose function seems to consist in helping others to practise patience, humility, charity, and every kind of Christian virtue. We may agree that there are no enemies in convents. Nevertheless it must sometimes happen that women—even nuns—who live together at close quarters, will take a hearty dislike to someone or other. There was no love lost between Mother M. de Gonzague and Pauline.

One such was Sister St. Peter, an arthritic, a helpless and cheerless old soul. No one could please her and even Teresa had to make a great effort to offer her services, and a greater one to get them accepted. Her task was to conduct the poor invalid to the refectory every evening at ten minutes to six. In the chapel Sister St. Peter gave the signal to start by shaking her sand-glass. Then Teresa had to move her stool, carry it in a particular way and, without hurrying, begin the journey. The stumbling, tottering and groaning old woman had to be supported by her girdle, very gently, and her companion had to listen to her grumblings: "Don't go so fast. I am going to fall; don't go so slow; where are you . . . I don't feel your hand. . . . You are letting go your hold. I knew you were too young to take care of me properly." The refectory was at last reached. Sister St. Peter was installed in her chair, her sleeves folded back, and her food cut up with a minute ceremonial which had to be observed carefully. Teresa ended her task by bestowing on poor old Sister St. Peter her sweetest smile. What self-mastery, what strength Teresa needed in order to go through this performance night after night without betraying her boredom and impatience by word or action, by slight indications of hurry, by a resigned or unnaturally sweet expression on her face or in her voice, than which nothing could be more exasperating! Instead of which she gave a cheerful obedience to the old woman's senseless directions, and finally, to crown it all, offered the royal gift of her sweet young smile.

The courage she had to summon, the self-control she achieved, can only be measured by her unconscious reaction at the end of it. For the first and only time she records in her biography a passing vision, soon extinguished, of the pleasures that might have been hers at that very same moment had she remained in the world. "One cold winter's evening, as I was leading Sister St. Peter from chapel to refectory, I thought I heard the harmonious strains of distant music, and there rose in my mind the picture of a rich ballroom brilliantly lighted and full of young girls elegantly dressed. Then I turned to the poor invalid; instead of music I heard her complaints, instead of rich gilding I saw the bare brick walls of our cloister scarcely visible in the dim flickering light." She felt she had something worth while to offer to her Lord and she rejoiced.

III. THE FORSAKING OF HUMAN AFFECTIONS
A RUTHLESS TERESA

The hardest sacrifices, the worst sufferings in the religious life, are not the material or physical ones. It is incomparably more difficult to renounce one's self than to renounce things. In the preceding pages we have seen how Teresa conquered her will and became meek and obedient under trying circumstances. We shall now see how she learned to do without human affections.

At home Teresa had been an affectionate child. She had been very fond of her mother and of Pauline and, in a lesser degree of her father and other sisters. She believed herself that she had an affectionate nature. "God has given me a faithful heart and when once I love, I love for ever." In reading the biography attentively it does not seem, however, that her loving disposition extended much beyond the family circle;

and at school her attempts at making friends either with the girls or with the mistresses were not very successful. Once she fixed her choice on two little girls of her own age as her particular friends. Alas! all the response she met with was a glance of indifference. Her friendship was not appreciated.[18] Nor was she more successful with the mistresses. Having observed that the sentimental advances of some girls to their teachers were not always unrequited, she tried to win favour in the same quarters and failed. After these attempts, making virtue a necessity, she gave up her quest for affections which were refused or proved inconstant. "How shallow are the hearts of creatures," exclaims Teresa in words that seem to express the wisdom and indifference of old age rather than the disappointments of a girl of twelve. "Happy failure, from how many evils have you not saved me! I am most thankful to our Lord that He has allowed me to find only bitterness in earthly friendships." She devotes more than a page to these considerations. One thing seems clear: at school she did not attract affection. They might have forgiven her for being a clever or even a good little girl, but who could stand a child so much given to weeping, and so odd in many ways; one who, at recreation time, did not take part in the games but watched the others from a distance, mooned or played alone?

In the family circle and among visitors it was agreed that Teresa was a pretty girl, and she herself, when she mentions it, does not deny this, not unpleasant, imputation. In the two untouched photographs of Teresa at fifteen, and at sixteen, one taken just before entering Carmel, the other on her clothing day, she appears as an intelligent, vivacious, decided young woman, with the plump and healthy face of a country girl; but our inexpert eyes failed to discover in these features anything that we could call beauty or even prettiness.

She was about twelve, and she had gone on holiday with her cousins to Trouville, when the conclusion was forced upon her that she did not possess the gift of attracting the loving

[18] E, p. 78.

attentions and endearments which other girls received as their due. She had noticed that her cousin Marie, who suffered from headaches, was, on these occasions, pitied and fondled and petted. One evening Teresa, in the hope of receiving the same caresses, threw herself into an armchair in a corner and began to cry and to moan feebly: "My head is aching." Nobody believed her and, instead of the expected petting, she was treated to a sound lecture. She remembered the fable of the lap dog and the donkey.[19] She was the donkey. She realized it did not suit her to *faire son intéressante* and to angle for sympathy. She was cured and never attempted again to try these feminine tricks on her friends. People endowed with a very strong will, as Teresa was, often inspire respect, devotion sometimes, affection very seldom, for they lack that softness and submissiveness that rouses the loving and protective instincts which most people feel towards the weak.

Her head was generally in full control of her heart. Once, however, she nearly succumbed to a craving for a love that was neither reasonable nor measured, but only too human. Soon after her arrival, the little postulant conceived for the Prioress one of those infatuations common enough among school girls of her age—she was fifteen—for one or other of their teachers. Describing how powerful was the attraction, Teresa tells us that it led her sometimes past the door of Mother de Gonzague. How much she wanted to knock at that door! "Pretexts for yielding to my natural affection suggested themselves in hundreds. I was so violently tempted to seek my own satisfaction, some crumbs of pleasure, by having a word with her, that I was obliged to hurry past her cell and cling to the banisters to keep myself from turning back." She conquered, she refused herself this consolation, and it does not seem that the same temptation ever came near her. Let us add that the conclusion of this episode was probably helped by the unexpected reaction of the Prioress to it. This emotional woman could not be ignorant for long of the

[19] *La Fontaine (Fables of)*, IV, 5.

sentiments of Teresa towards her, and her answer to this unwanted offer of affection was, as happens sometimes, some dislike for the child and a show of special severity towards her. A good discipline after all for the formation of Teresa! During the years that followed, in her relations with the rest of the community, in her treatment of the novices under her care, we find no trace of sentimental attachment on her side, and no echo of emotional friendship for her on the part of the others. Her sister Céline, giving evidence in view of her canonization, strikes the right note when she says: "We loved her very much, but none of us was tempted to feel for her this extreme and unreasonable affection which grows sometimes in those hearts which deceive themselves" (into mistaking it for Christian charity). This, translated into ordinary language, means that at the convent, after the first few years, they admired and respected her but never felt for her that warm, unreasoned human feeling which we call love.

"Had my eyes been dazzled by the deceitful light of creatures, I should have been utterly lost." Perhaps there is some exaggeration here, for she might not have been able to offer to "the creatures" the kind of love they wanted, even if she had wished it, and as a result her own feelings would have been neither appreciated nor returned. It seems to us also that, apart from this natural disability, sooner or later her exclusive and all-commanding desire to live for God, and love Him above all things, made it soon impossible for her to give any part of herself to human affections. In our hearts there is no room for two violent emotional states at the same time. One must conquer the other. "How can a heart given to human affection," she wrote, "be closely united to God?"

This is one of the reasons why, in convents, very close friendships, comforting as they would be to the individual, are very much discouraged. There are other considerations of a practical nature as well. In such a small world as a cloistered community must be, in such an uneventful life of routine as theirs is, the cliques and divisions, the jealousies and quarrels that particular friendships would occasion would make life intolerable for all. They must live for God and for Him forsake all deep attachments, to people as well as to material things.

* * *

The Story of a Soul gives us a definite impression that somehow in Teresa's character there was a hard streak, a ruthlessness where other human beings were concerned, and, since no one possesses an accurate and full knowledge of oneself, it is quite possible that she was not in the least aware of it. God builds the holiness of His saints with the materials at hand. By nature as well as by grace she may have found it easier than others—than Mother de Gonzague, for instance—to love those with whom she came in contact in a dutiful, measured and impersonal way.

In the pages that follow we must bear in mind that saints, who have constantly in their minds the thought of God, live on a plane where human ties, pleasures, sufferings are of no importance except in so far as they hinder or advance spiritual interests.

We are not trying to apportion the respective shares of grace and of nature in the attitude of Teresa towards others. We only register her sayings and actions as we find them in the autobiography. We shall not make much of the fact that she dwells more insistently and more often on her own sufferings than on those of others for, after all, she was writing her own story, not that of anyone else. But she does not seem to realize and take into account the pain she inflicted sometimes on other people.

In her decision to leave her house at fifteen, the thought of the distress her departure would cause her "old King" did not seem to occur to her. Her story is only concerned with the means of obtaining his consent, by tears first, then by persuasion and insistence. When she enters Carmel, he is in tears, but she is not. When, a year later, M. Martin has to be removed to a private asylum it is true that she says: "That since there are no words to describe her grief, she will not attempt to", but the words that follow, and which describe her feelings, are, to the ordinary person, amazing: "The three years of our dear father's martyrdom seem to me the sweetest and most fruitful of our lives. I would not exchange them for the most sublime ecstasies. . . . Though my suffering seemed to have reached its height . . . yet amidst these waters of tribulation I was the happiest of mortals."[20] She concludes this episode by telling us of its satisfactory results for her spiritual formation: "We no longer walked—we ran, we flew along the road of perfection."

She was fond of Céline, but when she hears of her going to a dance she prays earnestly that she may be prevented from taking any part in the dancing. The story is told at some length, and one feels she is almost gloating over the disappointment of the partner, a young man "who slipped away very much ashamed and did not dare appear again that evening". After Céline has joined her in Carmel, she does not mind whether her sister remains at Lisieux or goes to distant lands, and explains that her affection for her "was that of a mother rather than that of a sister", dutiful rather than sentimental. She had loved Pauline dearly, more than anyone in the world, even as a baby. Yet for five years, living in the same little convent, she deliberately refrains from having any private conversation with her. If it so happens that they are working together in the refectory, she will not say one word that has no bearing on their common work. In the pages written later on for Pauline she seems to complain: "Oh, my little mother, how much I suffered then. . . ." Did she not realize that Pauline, too, suffered? Teresa deliberately deprived herself of any kind of intimacy with her sister, but Pauline, whom she had not even taken into her confidence, did not understand it: "She wondered at this reserve and it pained her."

In all circumstances she took a spiritual, detached, reasonable view of suffering, whether her own or that of others.

[20] E, pp. 130-1.

When Pauline expressed sympathy for one of the Sisters who seemed exhausted, Teresa replied: " I do not feel as you do. Saints who suffer never excite my pity . . . their sufferings give glory to God."

When friends or relations called on her, she gave the Sisters a definite impression that she went to see them in the parlour only for charity's sake, through a feeling of duty. So they said after her death.[21]

Pauline, in the journal where she entered day by day her last conversations with Teresa in the infirmary, wrote the following memorandum which is perhaps more illuminating than our previous quotations.

She said to Teresa: " What would you have done if one of us three [her sisters] had been lying here sick instead of you? At recreation time would you have come to the infirmary, or joined the others at recreation? "

Answer: " I would have gone straight to recreation without asking any news of you, but I should have done it so discreetly that no one would think it was an act of abnegation."

Can it be right to treat as strangers the very ones whom nature, as well as God's commandment, bid us love like ourselves? When our Lord speaks of hating father and mother for His sake does it not mean that if a choice is forced on us we must be ready to sacrifice human love for the sake of God? It seems to us that Teresa's zeal outran her discretion.

We are supported in this interpretation by no less an authority than the foundress of the Carmel of Lisieux. Once, after the unbroken silence of a ten-day retreat, the Sisters were at last allowed to converse freely, but Teresa, when she joined the others at recreation, went and sat conspicuously right away from her sister Pauline without a single word of greeting. The venerable old Mother Genevieve thereupon reprimanded Teresa, saying she did not understand true charity. Most people, we think, will agree with her.

How often we have heard people apply to Teresa the debased adjective, sweet, and we have been taken aback by

[21] Petitot, p. 213.

such an unsuitable description. When she had decided on a course of conduct nothing could stop her, and the feelings of other people did not receive much consideration. At sixteen she was as sure of herself and as determined as if she had been the oldest nun in the community.

Being young, she was easily convinced she always knew what was right; being conscientious, she felt it was her personal duty to correct what she thought wrong. She informs us that at the beginning: "If I saw a Sister doing something I did not like and seeming contrary to our Rules, I used to think how glad I should be if I could only warn her and point out her mistake." It is quite possible that she did not always resist the impulse, and if so, found that the older women looked askance at this unsufferable child who made it her business to correct her elders. It is so difficult to harmonize zeal and prudence!

Some years later, she was given plenty of scope with the novices under her charge. By then, she had learnt the necessity of mixing diplomacy with firmness, but for all that even the novices sometimes returned her compliments with heavy interest.

She was entitled to say that "she did not worry about giving pain" and never flinched from inflicting a reprimand when it was needed. Even when physically enfeebled by illness, she found the strength to reprove a novice severely who had come to her with grievances, and vehemently insisted on her rights. The infirmarian, witnessing the scene, could not help saying to Teresa after the novice had gone: "What a vixen she is, would it not frighten you if she came again?" "A good soldier," answered the servant of God, "is not afraid of going to battle. Did I not say I would die sword in hand?"

Once, during these first two years, her criticism had for its target the very Prioress herself. When she entered Carmel, she found among the novices a companion some eight years older than herself, whose behaviour was in various ways a subject of regret and who seemed to entertain for their superior an affection that seemed more natural than spiritual.[22] Teresa had nursed such feelings towards the same woman a little while before, and now, with the understanding conferred on her by experience and with the zeal of a recent convert, she felt it her duty to put her erring sister right. She saw she must speak fearlessly or else end their pleasant but useless conversations. "She pointed out tenderly" to her senior that she must renounce this affection, for it was a form of self-love and she was only seeking her own pleasure. She won her point and we cannot help admiring the courage of this young girl in teaching a lesson both to an older companion and to the Prioress as well. "You may very well repeat to Reverend Mother everything I have told you. I would rather be turned out of the monastery by her than let you go astray and fail doing my duty." Brave words and braver action still, since she foresaw clearly their possible consequences. Recounting this episode seven years later, in pages dedicated to Mother Marie de Gonzague, the object of her warning, Teresa protested: "I had never intended turning away my companion from you. My aim was to explain to her that true love feeds on sacrifice, and that, as we renounce natural satisfactions, our affections become stronger and more unselfish." This strong action of Teresa, her indirect piece of advice to the head of the community, depriving her of the tender friendship of the young nun, cannot have sweetened the already strained situation between superior and novice, for no Prioress can be expected to relish the interference of a girl of sixteen. To her this may have smacked of impertinence and self-assurance and may explain partly the continuation of the severe treatment meted out to Teresa.

A few years later, in 1896, a similar rebuke was again inflicted by Teresa on Mother Marie de Gonzague, and this time publicly. We mention it here to avoid returning to the subject later on. Teresa was then twenty years old and was, under Mother Marie de Gonzague, a kind of companion and adviser to the novices. For purely personal reasons, Mother de Gonzague had decided to postpone the profession of two

[22] E, p. 174.

of them. This abuse of authority provoked discussions and recrimination among the nuns. Teresa, who, we may suppose, in conformity with the evangelical rule, had already made her protest privately to the guilty party, decided to make it publicly as well, and said: "This was the kind of ordeal that no Mistress of Novices has the right to impose on her charges." We must agree that public opposition to a woman given to scenes and exhibitions of temper required a good deal of courage. Teresa never forgot that fortitude was one of the seven Gifts of the Holy Ghost, and it was not the least remarkable side of her character.

IV. FINDING HERSELF

Even if one has decided to become a great saint, one cannot expect, in this prosaic world, that one will find ready at hand, waiting to be done, the shining deeds that will compel the admiration of mankind. Least of all would this be the case in a convent. Had Teresa harboured any such delusions, they would have been rudely shattered at the very start by some scathing remarks about cobwebs and brooms, or by a scornful reference to her disgraceful needlework, or an unfriendly comment about her lack of keenness about her duties.

Her ideal had long been Joan of Arc. She had longed to be a missionary and a martyr. She would have liked to be a priest, to say Mass and (she refers to it more than once) to preach. These longings belonged to that unprofitable company of day-dreams that have never solved any problem, least of all hers: how is one to become a great saint? By degrees she realized that the extraordinary ways of some saints, their long fasts and vigils, the excessive punishments they inflicted upon themselves, their visions, revelations and ecstasies, were not to be her way. Her holiness would be one within the reach of the millions whose lives are commonplace and uneventful, made up of obscure achievements, unimportant, unnoticed and unappreciated.

She did not succeed all at once. Influenced by the extreme ascetic notions of the Prioress and carried away by her own zeal, she at first tried exceptional measures that went beyond the Rule. Once she went on working with a sharp pin buried in her shoulder through someone's clumsiness. On another occasion she wore next to her skin a cross armed with spikes. The wounds festered and she had to be treated for them. She also gave a trial to the chains and nettles (for scourging) recommended by her extravagant Prioress. Acting on her own inspiration she chose to spoil her food by unpalatable additions of wormwood and other condiments of the same kind, until chronic indigestion recalled her to common sense. We may wonder why her confessor did not give some sensible advice on these short cuts to holiness, but, as we shall see presently, it is most unlikely that he ever heard of them through Teresa. She had to find out for herself that these singular practices were not for her and that there are other paths to perfection.

We might think that these exaggerated mortifications of the flesh are a survival of the old Manichaean spirit which saw evil in the most innocent pleasures, in beauty of shape, colour, or sound, in the perfume of flowers, and the sweet strains of music, for these heretics mistook the gifts of God for snares of the devil. This is not the Christian outlook and Teresa in the long run realized that penance is something quite different. It is a discipline to keep the body in subjection and make the spirit master in the house it inhabits; an expiation for the sins of those who do no penance, a redeeming sacrifice on behalf of sinners. No less clearly, like St. Bernard centuries before, she saw in the exaggerations that enfeeble the body an inverted form of self-indulgence and a spirit of singularity that fed one's secret pride.

She came to the conclusion that perfect observance of the rule was an effective and sufficient instrument of perfection for a nun. Let us make no mistake on this point. We said perfect observance, and this can be, in the long run, heroic.

Such is, for instance, obedience as Teresa practised it; constant obedience, exact obedience to rules of no particular importance, to people who seem unworthy of it, to orders that were unintelligent or inspired by caprice; obedience unrelieved by exceptions and privileges. Teresa did not interpret orders. She obeyed them, and to one of her wilful temperament this must have been particularly irksome. Let us give an example. We have alluded to her chronic indigestion when she was a postulant and a novice. She was given a specific order to tell the Mistress of Novices of these discomforts and, as it was a daily occurrence, she found this obligation very distasteful. The Mistress of Novices would exclaim, "The Rule is too hard for you, you will never stand it!" The Prioress, much displeased, would add, "That child is always complaining! If she cannot put up with her stomach-aches, she had better go." Teresa, however, out of obedience to an order long forgotten by the authority that had given it, continued, to the time of her profession, to come and tell the Mistress of Novices daily of her unpoetical complaints.

One may be allowed to wonder whether these digestive disturbances were due to an uncongenial diet or to Teresa's nervous temperament. In spite of what she says of her wonderful peace of mind, she may have worried much during these first two years in the convent, when she was still trying to find herself, to find her way, and to adapt herself to her new surroundings. That she felt the restrictions of a life confined within the narrow boundaries of the convent walls is very evident from the contents of her dreams. For dreams, the guardians of sleep, often fulfil our unconscious wishes, and bring us what we have been denied in our waking life. She says: "I think of God all through the day, but my mind does not dwell on Him in my sleep. As a rule I dream of woods and flowers, of brooks and the sea. I nearly always meet pretty children, or else chase birds or butterflies. . . . My dreams are sometimes poetical, they are never mystical."[23] Once she speaks of herself as a prisoner: "When I made

[23] E, p. 140.

myself a prisoner at the age of fifteen I gave up the delight of rambling through the meadows . . . etc."[24]

Coming back to our subject, it is probable that these unpleasant digestive troubles helped Teresa to discover the simple truth that, when one is in physical pain, or, as was the case with her, in chronic discomfort, one can give but an imperfect attention to spiritual things. An ordinary toothache will certainly confuse the serenity of a philosopher, and a pin in one's shoulder will effectually disturb the recollected frame of mind so necessary for meditation and prayer. Very sensibly she came to the conclusion that the keeping of the Rule, joined to the mortification of her will, pride and temper, would lead her safely to her goal.

The time soon came when she no longer spoilt her food deliberately, but took it as it was served, giving thanks to God when it was palatable, but welcoming an opportunity, when it was unsavoury, for self-denial.[25] In either event her command over herself was so perfect that no one, not even her sisters, could guess what she liked or disliked. She appeared always completely unaware of the quality of the food that was put before her.

The practice of silence is one that can be more arduous than any bodily penance, and more important, too, for without silence there can be no interior life. Many nuns, including the Prioress, took the view that the Rule, like the Law, is not concerned with trifles. One word or two, one minute or two, what did it matter? Teresa thought that it did, and kept the rule of silence to the letter and to the second. The others might exchange a greeting or a piece of news when they met on the stairs or in a passage. They might continue an interesting conversation for a few minutes after the bell had rung. If they were working together—even in the chapel—they might have a little chat, seeing no harm therein, but Teresa ended a conversation in the parlour, or at the end of the recreation, at the precise moment when the hour-glass gave the signal. She practised the silence which, in an argument,

[24] E, p. 144.   [25] N.V., p. 168.

left her in the wrong, the silence that could be misunderstood by her own sisters as indifference, by her companions as dullness of mind, by her superiors as an admission of guilt. A victory of this last kind—her first one—cost her, she said, a good deal. A small jar left in a passage was found broken. The Novice Mistress, thinking she was the culprit, reproached her for leaving it about, adding she was most untidy and in the future must be more careful. Without a word of self-defence, Teresa meekly promised to mend her ways, and kissed the ground. She adds in her biography that overcoming her pride in this way did her far more good than any bodily penance could have done. If anyone believes that this kind of silence, practised unfailingly at all times, is an easy and light thing, let him try it for twenty-four hours.

Teresa felt the cold very severely, particularly during the last two years of her life. Up to a point this could have been alleviated. She could, for instance, have asked for some extra blankets. But she did not, holding the view that this was a penance, not of her choice, not outside the Rule, and that she must accept it in the spirit of Carmel, in expiation of the crimes of a sinful world. In the same spirit, during the eight winters she spent in Carmel, she never betrayed by any sign that she was particularly sensitive to cold. One never saw her pinning up her sleeves or clutching up her dress close to her body as some Sisters did in the wind-swept cloister, or going about shrivelled up and bent double, in feigned misery. Instead she would walk straight and calm through the draughty passages in the convent, apparently unaffected by the temperature.

In monasteries all are bound by a vow of poverty which is as important for the welfare and discipline of the community as for the spiritual good of its members. One might say that in a monastery communism is practised more strictly than in any totalitarian country in the world, for monks or nuns have no private possessions; none of them can say, "this is mine," but they all say "our cell, our pen, our handkerchief, our shoes." When poverty is properly kept, everything in the monastery must be of the roughest, of the commonest description, and there must be no superfluities of any kind in garments or furniture or food. It is clear, however, that there is not much excellence in poverty by itself, even if we deliberately choose it; and none at all, if it is forced on us. Poverty is of itself no virtue. What makes it a Christian virtue is the *spirit of poverty*, a complete indifference to money, ownership, possessions of every kind. Teresa practised the poverty imposed by the Carmelite rule, but more important still she cultivated the spirit of complete detachment from all things. This explains some of her actions which otherwise would appear futile and fanciful. For instance, she snapped the glass head of a pin because it was pretty and she might have liked to keep it. She displayed such parsimony in the use of common things, eatables, writing materials, as might have passed in the world for extreme stinginess. But the spirit that inspired her actions was the wish to be as completely and absolutely poor as St. Francis of Assisi. It was not unkindness that caused someone to remove from Teresa's cell a pretty little jug and to replace it by an old unsightly one. It was the wish to ensure that she would not attach herself to it. Later on she taught the same lesson to a novice who had varnished the rough furniture of her cell. Teresa ordered her to scrub off this varnish, not that it was against the rules, but the novice might have become attached to her scanty possessions and thought of them as hers.

* * *

Roughly speaking, the day of a Carmelite at Lisieux comprised some six hours of prayer and five of work. Mass and the Divine Office occupied three of those six hours, while meditation, spiritual reading and instructions filled up the rest. Compare the time given to prayer and that allotted to manual work, and you measure the relative importance of prayer and work in the life of the nuns.

We are not going to venture on the uncharted seas of

mystical speculation—we leave this to specialists—but we may perhaps safely say that Teresa, being a natural contemplative, must have reached at an early date the stage when she was at all times aware of the presence of God and let her mind and heart dwell on Him in a continuous and almost unconscious union. Here we are only concerned with the known reactions and responses of Teresa to the devotional exercises of the community before her Profession.

The Mass, sacrifice and sacrament, is for a Catholic the supreme act of worship, besides which all private prayers sink into insignificance. In the Mass, which is a continuation of the Passion, Christ Himself, priest as well as victim, offers to His Father such adoration, praise and atonement as are beyond the powers of man. Holy Communion, an integral part of the sacrifice, is the sacrament which gives the communicants some kind of participation in the holiness and the divinity of the victim.

St. Teresa, to whom the Real Presence and Holy Communion meant so much, has little to say in her autobiography about the Mass as a sacrifice, as an act of adoration and of praise. As a child she found it impossible to follow the prayers of Mass in her prayer book, so that she had to be called to order, and her companions at school accused her of not attending Mass properly. If she was shown how to follow it in her book she acknowledged this by a smile, looked at the page for a few seconds, and then looked away. It is probable that the prayers contained in her *Paroissien* were those of Fénelon, written in a noble and vague language that meant little to a child (this at least was our own experience), and Teresa found it best to pray in her own way. At the convent, we take it for granted that she would have been expected to follow the Mass by reading the same liturgical prayers which priest, bishop or Pope reads at the altar. It is quite possible that the lack of sentimental appeal of the prayers of the Missal, even of those that come before and after Communion, and of the official thanksgiving (the last Gospel) may have disappointed Teresa. We might almost say deterred, for she

POSTULANT AND NOVICE

was very sensitive to any insistence on divine justice and punishment, and the Missal prayers make quite a few references to the uncertainty of our salvation.[26]

Nuns, as a rule, are not liturgically minded. The dignified, but unemotional statements of the liturgy do not appeal to them. They are more baffled than satisfied by the simplicity and matter-of-factness of the Communion prayers in the Missal. The prayers they write themselves for the edification of the public contain little doctrine, but overflow with sentiment. Usually they do not seem to attach the same importance to the idea of Sacrifice, as to that of sacramental Communion.

The devotion of Teresa to the sacrament of the Eucharist was remarkable. When, as a child, she saw her sisters approach the Holy Table, she wondered whether it would be lawful for her, unbidden and unnoticed, to accompany them. Her preparation for First Communion was lengthy and thorough to a degree. Afterwards, when her confessor, unasked, allowed her to receive Communion several times a week—a most unusual practice in those days—her joy was great. When at the convent she found this privilege parsimoniously measured according to Mother Prioress' whims, her disappointment was correspondingly severe. She prized Communion above all things and it is with regret that she had to record truthfully that she often fell asleep both during meditation and thanksgiving after Communion,[27] and also "that there was no time when she had less consolation than during her thanksgiving". We can look upon this as a valuable contribution to her spiritual outlook and training. Had she had these "consolations" it would have been easy for one of her temperament to mistake an emotional satisfaction for love of God.

Teresa made up on a grand scale for what she considered as a lack of response on her part by continuing her thanksgiving throughout the day, and for this we must admire her.

We must confess, however, that we cannot find so admirable some actions of Teresa which, under an appearance of

[26] Petitot, p. 187.   [27] E, p. 134.

devotion, look more like the irresponsible whim of a child than the deliberate act of a grown-up woman. As a novice she shared with another the task of cleaning the chapel. Once, when they were both at work together, this novice saw Teresa make a genuflexion before the altar and knock on the door of the tabernacle, saying, "Art Thou there, Jesus? I beseech Thee to speak to me." She stayed for some seconds with her head against the tabernacle and then turned to her companion "with a face transfigured and shining with joy". Whether the novice at the time perceived this transfiguration as clearly as she did fifteen or twenty years later, when rumours of canonization were in the air, is open to question. Of one thing we are convinced, however, and it is this: had Teresa four years later caught one of her novices playing these pious pranks in the chapel, she would have chided her with the same earnestness as any parish priest if he found the ladies of the parish on the altar steps indulging in this kind of religious exercise. Teresa was only sixteen at the time, and was possibly influenced by a pious picture then very popular, that of a baby crawling on the table of the altar and knocking at the door of the tabernacle. Anyway, we can only look at this episode as a childish indiscretion. Teresa was still feeling her way towards her goal and had to find it by the common process of trial and error.

Of her meditations we know one thing. She could not assimilate the ordinary methods such as that of St. Ignatius, or even the very simple and logical one of St. Francis of Sales. It is probable that she found plans, systems, and methods uncongenial to her turn of mind and decided to give herself to purely contemplative meditation as the Spirit moved her.

The recitation of the Divine Office occupied some two hours every day, and gave the saint great happiness. Rightly so, since the Office is made up for the greatest part of Psalms. These are the inspired prayers written by the prophets, sung by our Lord Himself and chosen by the Church, from the earliest days of her existence, for the clergy and divine services, as both the ideal and traditional form of prayer. Teresa took great delight in saying the Office, and perhaps the imagery, the directness, the austere and pure spiritual doctrine may have been responsible for her poor opinion of other books of devotion. Wrapping up in words of praise her dislike of them all, she wrote: "These collections of lovely prayers, each one more beautiful than the next! Such a multitude of them that I cannot pick out the best and so must pray in my own way." More bluntly and truthfully she adds that these beautiful prayers gave her a headache! We may possibly agree heartily with this verdict, when we read her own unbearably emotional compositions.[28] Her judgment was not at fault. It is quite true that a good many printed prayers (not excluding by any means those written by saints) are too often empty of everything except good intentions and sentiment. Perhaps the best prayers, as long as we model them on the lines of the Lord's prayer, are those we make up for ourselves. Teresa found it so: "I must pray in my own way!"

The reading of spiritual books is part of the curriculum of a convent. Here, also, Teresa was feeling her way and looking out for the spiritual fare that best suited her temperament. Our mind, like our body, is allergic to certain foods and no two individuals are quite alike in this respect. She had no affinity, for instance, with the mind of a St. Francis of Sales, a genius so eminently French in his practical, clear and logical spirituality enlivened by an amused and spontaneous wit. His treatise on the love of God, untouched by emotional raptures, could have meant but little to her. She much preferred the obscure and ardent poetry of St. John of the Cross. At an early age she had discovered the *Imitation of Christ*, and her uncommon maturity of mind seems to have been attuned to this exquisite book. Later on in Carmel, apart

---

[28] See the prayers collected at the end of Pauline's *Novissima Verba*—"Prayers to the Holy Face" for example. "O my Beloved, for Thy love, I accept not to see here below the sweetness of Thy countenance, not to feel the inexpressible kiss of Thy mouth, but I implore Thee to set me on fire with Thy love, so that it may consume me rapidly and that I may soon appear before Thee: TERESA OF THE HOLY FACE."

from that book and from the writings of St. John of the Cross, the Holy Scriptures became the main foundation and nourishment of her spiritual life. She was in constant and immediate contact with them and we find an echo of her enthusiasm in such declarations as these: "It is in the Scriptures that I receive all my poor soul needs." "I can find nothing in books any more. The Gospel is enough for me." Soon, she knew by heart many pages of the Gospel, and we find in her works more than 400 quotations taken from the Old and the New Testaments.

One cannot expect her quotations to be learned or critical for it was enough for her that they should nourish her piety. She often gives them a meaning that one cannot link up with the original, and as often as not they are irrelevant to the occasion. Their choice seems at times guided by some emotional need, for she relates most texts to herself, even some which, by the nature of their contents, seem applicable only to our Lord. We are alluding here to a long fragment of the XVIIth chapter of St. John's Gospel, the moving words of farewell of our Lord at the last supper.[29] Even if one leaves out some lines found in the English translation of Mgr. T. Taylor (. . . *that they may be one, as we also are one. . . . That they may see my glory which Thou hast given me because Thou hast loved me before the foundation of the world*), enough remains to make one pause and wonder. People who have read those words in their context in the gospel until they know them by heart, who have pondered over them in meditation or in thanksgiving, and now find them appropriated by Teresa for her own purposes, will perhaps feel uneasy at this unwonted use of the sacred text.

In noting down our impressions of Teresa at this stage we are offering neither praise nor criticism, but only recording the facts. Every saint—and perhaps every thinking human being—is unique and original and must find his way alone, a way that is his own and not that of anyone else.

* * *

[29] E, Chap. XII, p. 191. In the 1953 French edition, Chap. X, p. 156.

POSTULANT AND NOVICE

This leads us to the question of spiritual direction, and here again we shall give facts rather than opinions.

We have already had occasion to quote her statement that with regard to confession "she did not feel the need of any other guide but Jesus". Speaking of the reading of Holy Scripture, and specially of the Gospels, she states[30] that "I find in their pages all the lights my poor soul needs . . . and I know and have experienced . . . that our Master has no need of book or teacher to instruct a soul", a doctrine which, taken too literally, might authorize Protestants to claim St. Teresa as a champion of private judgment, just as G. B. Shaw claimed St. Joan as an early Protestant. Her statements may appear sometimes a bit unguarded.

Père Petitot tells us that she had confessors, but not at any time a spiritual director. This, as we shall see, is a very correct estimate.

We should bear in mind that Teresa as a child was handicapped by a nervous timidity which, even had she had at her command the necessary vocabulary, would have made it practically impossible for her to explain to confessors the doubts, emotions and difficulties that filled her mind. Add to this an original and wilful disposition which made it difficult for her to ask for advice or accept it if uncongenial. Let us remember how she felt about Marie, her eldest sister, after she had discouraged the plan to enter Carmel at fifteen. We do not think that she told her confessor of her intention to do so nor asked for his opinion. If he had agreed, she would not have kept it a secret, and if he had not, we should have heard another tale of despair and tears.

When she felt the imperious need of advice she went to Marie, her eldest sister, and poured into her ears a tale of scruples and of the misery they caused her. Marie and Pauline were the only people to whom it was possible to open her heart freely, and, after she had entered Carmel, she found herself, at least for a time, thrown upon her own resources. In convents, and specially at that date before the Papal

[30] E. p. 147.

instruction on "the manifestation of conscience" had been issued, nuns were expected to come to their Mother Superior for spiritual advice and "to open their conscience to them", a custom which was easily open to abuse. Novices had, besides, to act similarly with their Mistress of Novices, so that chaplains, apart from hearing the actual confession and giving absolution, had little to do in the way of direction. A chaplain is no more a prophet in his convent than a rector in his parish and the nuns in need of direction would not go to him but to Mother Superior, even if she was as unbalanced as Mother de Gonzague or as simple as Sister Marie des Anges.

Teresa was not very happy in her superiors. We have not forgotten that from the start all the spiritual advice she received from the Prioress, on the rare occasions when she was granted an interview, was an hour of scoldings unrelieved by any practical advice. As for the Mistress of Novices, this good but unintelligent woman (the same one that killed the devil with a stick in the courtyard) is also the one who told the Roman tribunal of the "majesty" of the little postulant. It is improbable that, with the best will in the world, she could have given much profitable advice to a girl of that stamp. Teresa, using the same charitable expressions as she did towards the Prioress, tells us that "much as I loved and appreciated her my soul did not expand under her guidance. Words failed me when I spoke and my time of spiritual direction became a torture and a real martyrdom."[31]

It is perhaps a pity she could not open her mind to her confessor for, as we are going to see, it appears that her scruples continued after she had become a postulant. A firm and sensible director could have given her great assistance. The chaplain had every reason to know what kind of woman the Prioress was, and had he been consulted he would have discouraged the singularities and the extreme forms of mortification favoured by her at the beginning. Teresa, however, did not find it easy or necessary to ask for advice and might have argued and resented any that did not agree with her own

[31] E, pp. 122, 124.

opinions. Are we exaggerating here? Far from it. This is, in fact, what happened and we have it from Teresa herself.

Her attitude towards confession is perhaps best illustrated by an anecdote which was repeated by one of the novices who had it from Teresa herself. The episode to which it refers probably belongs to her fourteenth year. "If I had not been received into the Carmel," she said, "I should have entered a Refuge and lived there unknown and despised among the poor 'penitents'. My joy would have been to be taken for one of them and be an apostle among them," etc. "But how could you have hidden your innocence from your confessor?" said the novice. "I should have told him that while still in the world I made a general confession, and that it was forbidden me to repeat it."[32]

This deserves some attention, for they were not the irresponsible words of a little girl, but the considered view of Teresa at twenty or more, and she was in the same mind as at fourteen on this point. The only comment we can offer is that the story gives us a good picture of the reticence—to put it mildly—which Teresa observed with her confessor. What direction could she have received from someone whom she intended misleading to this extent? The very reluctance of Teresa to open her mind, to ask for advice or to accept it without arguing, created in the confessor a corresponding reserve. One does not like to offer counsel where it is not wanted. Teresa tells us that she tried to be as an open book to her superiors, but with her own confessor she failed to succeed. If one advised her to moderate her ambitions—meaning, we may suppose, to take one step at a time and not to do anything extraordinary—she would answer that it was right to wish to be a great saint because our Lord himself had said: "Be perfect as your Father in heaven is perfect." Once the chaplain told her, "Do not let your mind dwell on your doubts. It is dangerous," and she told her sisters, "You see how little consolation I get."

"I have received no encouragement from anyone," she

[32] E, p. 297.

said, "but from Pauline. When occasion offered, when I could have opened my conscience, I was so little understood that, like St. John of the Cross, I said to God: 'Do not send me any more messengers unless *they can say to me what I want.*'"[33] She found the messenger she desired in Father Pichon, S.J., to whom she made a general confession. The account of it, as given by Teresa, sounds very strange when we consider that Père Pichon was a man of experience and Teresa a child of fifteen. She states that he was "astonished at the workings of grace in her soul" and as soon as her confession was finished he declared solemnly: "Before God, the Blessed Virgin, the Angels, and all the Saints, I declare that you have never committed a mortal sin." She does not tell us the reason he had for making this statement, which sounds as imprudent as it would have been unnecessary with an ordinary penitent; she seems to have taken it simply as a tribute to her exceptional perfection; if, however, we give credit to Père Pichon for ordinary prudence and common sense, and remember also that for years Teresa had been tormented by scruples, the need for such a declaration becomes obvious. Teresa tells us that, as usual, "she felt an extreme difficulty to open her heart". Every confessor will understand at once what she meant by this "extreme difficulty", as unpleasant for him as for the scrupulous penitent. He saw her at once as one of those victims of scruples whose unprofitable and needless anxieties cannot be dispelled by argument, and, using all the authority he could summon, gave her the comforting assurance that in her long recital of imaginary mortal sins he had not found a single one that deserved this name.

His next piece of advice was this. "May our Lord always be your superior and your novice master." Did he realize that she was going to add mentally: Let Him be my Director too? and that, in fact, it was the line she had always consistently followed. There is, however, this to be said in justification of this advice: on the one hand he was well

[33] Petitot, p. 190.

POSTULANT AND NOVICE 113

aware of the erratic and often irrational ways of the Prioress and he had also soon taken the measure of the good but not overbright Mistress of Novices: on the other hand he realized the sincerity and clear intellect of Teresa as well as her masterful nature. Seeing which way the Holy Spirit was moving this particular soul, he decided at once to encourage and not to hinder. This time Teresa had at last found a confessor *who told her what she wanted*, that she need not expect spiritual direction from confessors or superiors.

She never saw Father Pichon again. He had done his work, and there was little else he could have added, for Teresa was one of those few souls who can stand alone and only want confirmation that they are on the right road.

Three years later she was to meet another confessor, Father Alexis, who understood her. We shall speak of this at the proper time.

* * *

These two years as postulant and novice must have been particularly trying to one of the bringing up and character of Teresa. We have in mind less the physical conditions of her new life than the new and hard training to which she submitted her mind and will. At home she had never been accustomed to wait upon herself or to do any household work.[34] Here she must give some five hours daily to rough and uninteresting occupations. At home, if she happened to make her own bed or render some little service, she expected profuse praise and thanks. Here she received no applause, only reprimands and rebuffs. Formerly, it is true, she never complained or grumbled, but she had found out that a woman rules a household more easily by tears than by scenes and nagging. In Carmel, she no longer used weeping as a means of softening people's hearts, and accepted an unjust scolding without any sign of resentment and without any attempt at justification.

[34] E, p. 83.

H

By the end of her novitiate the main lines of her spiritual life were already laid down. Not for her the extraordinary bodily penances of the saints in past ages. She had tried them and found, as many did before her, that they made her unfit for anything else. Not for her the privileges of many great saints: visions and revelations. Hers would be a way of obscurity, of self-effacement, so that when she lay dying some sister would exclaim: "What could one say of her? She keeps the Rules well, but she has never done anything worth the telling." (By the way, what a fine epitaph for a saint, and what perfect humility it suggests!) Her manner of achieving holiness would be founded on the constant practice of insignificant and unnoticed little sacrifices, small acts of virtue, within the reach of everyone. This is not so easy as it looks. During these two years she found "that even trifles cost her dear", and had to encourage herself with the thought that all would come to light on the day of judgment.

How should we, at this date, sum up the general opinion of the community? Did they already visualize her as a future saint of the calendar? Some two or three testimonials, composed many years later in anticipation of an approaching canonization, should, in our opinion, be examined cautiously, because they are contradicted by common experience and by some otherwise known facts. We should say that, at the beginning, the nuns would reserve their judgment. The child was certainly eager and kept the rules meticulously, but then most beginners make a good start. At times they may have found her irritating, for her very excess of zeal stood in their way as a reproach. After a while they would note that there was no falling off, no relaxation of her minute observance of all the Rules. Her firmness on one or two occasions had been noticed and probably very differently judged, but otherwise she was quiet, pleasant to everybody, though not trying to make friends. She never complained, allowed everyone to make use of her, in short, seemed unimportant and did not attract attention in any way. She had even some little weaknesses, involuntary ones, that seemed to keep her down to the common level, such as being extremely slow at work, or falling asleep during meditation. They even thought sometimes that she was not keen in performing the duties allotted to her. Briefly, they saw in her nothing very much out of the ordinary and she was, for them, just a little postulant, just a little novice, unnoticeable and unnoticed.

CHAPTER V

A FULLY FLEDGED CARMELITE

1. TERESA TAKES HER VOWS

TERESA had been looking forward to the day of her Profession when she would be allowed to bind herself for ever to poverty, chastity and obedience, and her eagerness had still been sharpened further by a delay of eight months imposed on her by Canon Delatroëtte, the ecclesiastical superior of the convent. He thought her too young for taking such an irrevocable step.

At last the great day drew near, but, during the retreat that preceded the taking of her vows, a reaction set in. She went through a state of utter desolation, "seemingly abandoned by God",[1] and, on the eve of the ceremony, her belief that she had a vocation for the religious life appeared to her as a figment of her own imagination. "She was wholly unsuited for the Carmelite way of life; she had no real call to it and was deceiving her superiors."[2] This last-minute panic was not due, you will notice, to the very natural fear that a young woman might experience, on the eve of taking vows so completely at variance with all human inclinations, the fear that, some time in the long years ahead, she might regret her decision. With Teresa this was not the question at all. This was not her fear. She doubted whether she was good enough for the high vocation she was about to embrace. The Novice Mistress to whom she confided her scruples had no hesitation, laughed at these unfounded fears, and completely reassured her.

Teresa pronounced her vows on September 8th, 1890, and

[1] E, p. 134.   [2] E, p. 135.

A FULLY FLEDGED CARMELITE 117

took the veil a fortnight later. She had at this time already spent nearly two years and a half in the convent and would be eighteen on January 2nd of the following year. Her Profession made her a permanent member of the Order of Carmelites, and from now on neither could she withdraw nor could the Prioress send her away. It is true she never took her place among the other professed nuns in the Chapter, to give her opinions on the affairs of the community, but this was, partly at least, because the Rule did not allow more than two Sisters to sit on the Council of the monastery.[3] To the end, though professed, she remained among the novices.

She had already been observing all the rules of the Order, and in this respect her Profession made no change in her life, but we should explain here what her duties were after she had made her Profession. She left the linen room, where she had been working for two years, and was put in charge of the refectory, having to sweep and dust it. She had to see to the distribution of bread, water and beer, the latter being a bitter decoction of hops prepared by the Sisters themselves. For one year (1891-92) she was in charge of the sacristy. After June 1892, she did some painting in the chapel and helped the Sister in charge of the stores. From then on, until the elections of 1896, she was *Tourière*, that is, the Sister in charge of the *Tour*, a revolving hatch through which parcels and communications from outside entered the convent. She continued also to attend to all decoration and painting where it was needed and in the chapel especially. From February 1893 until she died she was also helping Mother de Gonzague with the training of the novices under the unofficial designation "Companion of the Novices". In March 1896, when Mother de Gonzague was elected Prioress, Teresa became sacristan once more and kept this charge until her health broke down altogether. She gave most of these details to her sister Pauline, who has recorded them in *Novissima Verba*.[4]

---

[3] See also a remark we made previously on this point.
[4] N.V., pp. 73-4.

II. LOVE ONE ANOTHER

Teresa, during the first three or four years she had spent in Carmel, had almost grown to her full spiritual stature, i.e., before the end of 1891. Very occasionally one notices some injudicious actions, such as kissing the altar breads to be used at Mass, or some indiscreet manifestations of zeal, such as the ostentatious care she took to avoid the company of her sisters. But now that we are dealing with the professed nun, we have no longer before us the girl of thirteen who is violently upset when she does not get her own way, and sheds tears of despair when Leo XIII tells her that the will of God will be done. By now she has harnessed her immense will power to the service of obedience. She is past the stage when, as a novice, she was making groping experiments in the ways to holiness. By now she has found her way and her only business is to press on unflinchingly. We have before us a woman who is sure of herself. She practises the same virtues as before but with more certainty and serenity.

Spiritual progress, the eventless life of a contemplative nun in a convent, are surely not the materials which suggest to the writer, and promise to the reader, an exciting story. It is true that the novelist, M. van der Meersch, turned it into a drama of some power, but he could do this only at the cost of historical truth. The drama is there, for Teresa says that "not a day passed without a struggle, not one", but it is an invisible one. The endless conflicts of Teresa with herself, and with the painful problems created by her own nervous condition, were all secret, all interior, ones. She never spoke of them and invariably offered to the Sisters a countenance of calm, smiling peace. All we know is only what she has chosen to tell us in her autobiography.

The real difficulties of her life are not to be sought for in the physical hardships—real as they are—of convent life;

nor are the three vows taken on the day of Profession the intolerable burden the world imagines. The scrupulous observance of these vows makes them, in the long run, not only bearable but easy and even pleasant. The *Cella continuata dulcescit* of the *Imitation* is as true now as it was seven hundred years ago. Long custom gives sweetness even to solitude. More irksome are some circumstances of convent life which outsiders seldom suspect. Obedience under a kindly and lovable superior is a very light burden, but what of the lack of close friendships, the lack of ready sympathy and understanding that only a bosom friend can supply? What of the lack of those little bits of gossip, of those little secrets that most women love to exchange with one another at any hour of the day? Above all, what of those house companions whom you can neither avoid nor take a liking to, for whom perhaps you feel a natural aversion and to whom you are bound for life?

Apart from her interior difficulties, with which we shall deal presently under the title of "sufferings", the main problem which confronted Teresa was that of her relations with that mixed society found in a convent of twenty to twenty-five women who have in common the same religious vocation, but very little else. Some may be rough, tactless, uneducated, while others are refined, pleasant, cultured. They may not all be charitable at all times; tempers become frayed, and a verbal warfare, subdued and softened as it may be by a strong religious outlook, is sure to be waged occasionally. Peace of the heart in the midst of strife, through likes and dislikes, is as necessary to spiritual life as it is difficult to retain. Teresa had her own dislikes. She may even have felt something like aversion towards some of her companions, and she may have been tempted to adopt the easy solution and to avoid them or keep them at a distance. Even saints are human. But, knowing that it is a poor kind of religious life that concentrates upon oneself as if the rest of mankind did not exist, she grappled, as a saint alone could do it, with this big problem. We are now going to see what prodigies of tact, diplomacy and Christian charity she displayed in interpreting the precept "Love one another".

* * *

We have not very far to seek in order to discover how Teresa understood and practised the virtue of charity. In the tenth chapter of her *Story of a Soul*[5] (The New Commandment), and in the eleventh (The Novice Mistress), she explains it at some length. In the former she tells us how she dealt with the other professed nuns, her equals, and, in the second, with her subordinates, the novices.

She lays down the general principles, she says, that true charity consists in bearing with one another's defects, in not being surprised at their mistakes but rather attributing good intentions to everyone as far as possible, and in taking notice of their smallest virtues.

"Judge not," says the Gospel. "How could we," concluded Teresa, "since we cannot read clearly other people's minds?" And she gives us a personal illustration.

One day the portress came during recreation and asked for a Sister to help her in some particular task. Teresa would have enjoyed it, and, as it happened, was chosen for it. She began to fold up her needlework, but did this very slowly so as to give a chance to another Sister, who, like herself, was desirous to do this particular piece of work. The portress, noticing how slow Teresa was, said laughingly: "I knew you did not want to add this pearl to your crown and that is why you were so slow." Everyone shared that impression; they all misjudged her.

"Love your enemies," commanded our Lord, and Teresa comments: "In a convent there are no enemies," but, as everywhere else, one may find there some unlovable people who make life unpleasant for others, who are touchy, inconsiderate, tactless. Teresa called them "imperfect souls" and remarks that "their company is avoided and they are usually

[5] E, p. 164.

left alone". She was, like everyone else, tempted to go a long way round to avoid meeting them. But to run away from people is not love nor a sign of love. "This one that I dislike," she writes, "is the one that I must love even though she makes it evident she does not care for me. It is not enough to love. I must prove it." And she proved it so well that one of the "imperfect souls" wondered at the smiles she received, and asked Teresa: "Would you tell me what it is that seems to attract you towards me so strongly?" Perhaps the saint overacted the part this time, for the Sisters were taken in and remarked on it.

This was her usual line of conduct with those for whom she had a natural dislike. She treated them as if they were cherished friends. If she had a conversation with them, she would not contradict nor enter into a verbal contest, no matter what they said. If she was tempted to give a disagreeable answer, she would keep silence, smile and perhaps change the conversation. If the temptation to argue became irresistible, she would slip away quietly "like a deserter from the battlefield".

In the Sermon on the Mountain, our Lord gave His listeners the following advice: "Give everyone that asketh thee; of him that taketh away thy goods, ask them not again. . . . If any man take away thy coat, let go also the cloak with him." How right, and how easy this should be in a convent! Since no one owns anything, how could one claim back something that does not belong to him? In the world, a literal interpretation of this precept would lead to unsocial results and be an injustice to one's dependants; but in a monastery private property does not exist, and no one can say, *my* book, *my* box of paints, *my* lamp or *my* brush. Why is it, she thought, that one cannot stifle without much effort a natural hankering after private ownership? For instance, she says: "When I am starting to paint, if I happen to find the brushes in confusion, if a ruler or penknife be missing, I am sorely tempted to lose patience and I have to resist a strong impulse to demand, and this sharply, the missing articles. It is lawful for me to ask for them but I should beg, like the poor who do not expect anything as a right but only as a gift."

Continuing to analyse motives and temptations, Teresa considers the question of borrowing. Frequently people speak of borrowing because this metaphor saves their pride. They have no intention of returning the loan, and under the cover of that word they escape the sense of obligation they would otherwise incur. When such a "borrower" comes to us, it seems hard to pretend one does not see through the deception. A Sister, well known for her failure to repay loans of time or work, comes to you, says Teresa, and talks of borrowing; your first impulse is to answer: "I will *give* you what you ask." The remark would gratify your own pride, as it is more generous to give than to lend. In addition it would let the Sister know you are not taken in by her little deception.

It is at least as difficult to give oneself, one's time and attention and courtesy as to let go the coats and cloaks the Gospel takes for examples. In Carmel the Sisters often asked for one another's benevolent help in their respective tasks, and exchanged little services. In these trifling transactions one can exhibit a spirit of charity or the reverse. Teresa enters into some points of detail. Which is best, she wondered, to offer one's help spontaneously or to wait until it is asked for? Well, she thought, it is more pleasant to give without being asked, but less meritorious, since it is something we have chosen to do of our own accord.[6] And, step by step, Teresa analyses the various degrees of charity displayed in the manner of giving. We find it easy to grant a favour if it has been asked courteously, but we are offended, perhaps inwardly rebellious, if tactless words have been used. Too often, in giving, we make imaginary difficulties in order to set off our generosity. We make it clear with many words that we are granting a favour and that the recipient must not presume and take it as a right.

More precious still than our time or services, and more truly ours, are the fruits of our mind, a clever thought, a witty

[6] One could find equally good reasons also for the opposite view.

remark, a well-turned story, and it is extremely galling to find that someone has appropriated them without acknowledging their source. When this trick was played on Teresa it seemed to her that they were taking something that was hers, that it was a theft, and yet, she says, "Why should not that Sister regard these thoughts or sayings as her own? The thought came to them from me, but to them and to me it had been sent by the Holy Spirit, freely and as a gift."

III. COMPANION OF NOVICES

In order to understand more fully what Teresa meant by loving one's neighbour, we must turn to her dealings with the novices she had under her care, not indeed as a mistress, but as a companion, for the fuller title remained the possession of Mother Marie de Gonzague. Her position was a very delicate one and called for the exercise of much discretion. She had to deal on one hand with a temperamental Mistress of Novices inclined to make scenes about nothing, and on the other, with young women who were of the same age or older than herself. Teresa was no more than twenty at the time of her appointment, but her strong personality soon gave her the share of authority that had not been granted officially.

She had observed that only love can make authority acceptable and correction fruitful, but she knew also that a purely human affection would not serve her purpose. Keeping in mind that her aim was to draw their hearts to God, not to herself, and that no good could come from self-seeking, she offered them a love entirely detached from self, a love that expected no return, no human gratification, none of the sweet pleasures of friendship.

Acting on this principle "she never shunned the unpleasant duty of telling a truth that would hurt". Some of the novices found her so hard that for a time they would have nothing more to do with her. They would even turn on her sharply and answer criticism by criticism in a language that, once at least, reminded her of the curses of Semei against David.[7] As they were all about the same age, and she had no official authority over them, they would on occasion serve her with what Teresa calls "a salad well seasoned with vinegar" and with utter frankness explain what they disliked in her. It seems to us that, although she protests she loved "her little lambs" and would have laid down her life for them, this impersonal love of hers, as clear as a winter sun, and as cold, sometimes repelled the novices more than it comforted them. In the end, they always came round, for they knew that Teresa had their good at heart, that her remarks were justified and that, selfless as it was, her love for them was real. Sometimes they even thanked her for her corrections.

We may regret very much that one or two of those novices did not keep a diary and write down a daily record of their conversations. We should have found a more lively and many-sided account of Teresa in documents contemporary with the events than in the syrupy recollections offered to the public twenty or thirty years later; the celestial looks, the transfigured face, the inspired accents, which in earlier days they had not yet discovered.

Teresa was never at a loss for words, and we have already reported that the throat trouble from which she began to suffer in 1895 was attributed by public consent to her endless conversations with the novices. Sometimes she thought herself inspired because it happened that she guessed what they were thinking before she was told. We may, however, be allowed to suggest that, considering she lived with her young charges, that they were together the whole day, that it was her business to observe them and to be on the alert, she would have been a singularly unobservant, if not obtuse woman, had she failed to notice when there was something seriously amiss with one of them.

Even during her last weeks of illness she went on advising and reprimanding them. In its proper place we shall mention some of the interviews they had with her in the infirmary.

[7] E, p. 182.

IV. TERESA AND THE HOLY EUCHARIST

Her devotion to the Holy Eucharist had a paramount place in her life. Jansenist influences had not entirely died out after two centuries, even in convents, and daily Communion was an almost unknown practice in the world outside. Teresa, even before she entered Carmel, had voiced her desire for more frequent Communion. In the convent she received it as often as she was permitted by the Prioress. During her last illness, before she was sent to the infirmary, she would rise after a sleepless night of coughing, even after some painful treatment, leave her little cell, and attend Mass in the chapel that she might have Communion.

It was faith, not sentimental considerations alone, that made her desire it so strongly. We have already had occasion to point out that, during the days of her novitiate, she confessed that there was no moment when she received less consolation than during her thanksgivings. Later on, she added that this was true not only of her early days in Carmel but always. And because distractions, drowsiness and sleep overcame her at that time of the morning, she often took the resolution to continue her thanksgiving throughout the day. This practice is not unknown among pious layfolk, but in view of this resolution of Teresa, Père Petitot goes further and, hesitatingly feeling his way, he puts forward a curious conjecture. He quotes Teresa as saying, "I cannot receive Communion as often as I wish, but, Oh Lord, are you not All-Mighty? Remain in me as in a tabernacle, never stay away from your little host." Then he quotes Pauline, "*I am sure* that Teresa was not thinking then of the permanence of the divine influence (?) which occurs without miracle in the faithful soul, but of the miraculous permanence of the consecrated elements." She affirms that she is sure this was what Teresa was thinking but gives no proofs, no reasons, for her certainty. Père Petitot goes further and seems to infer that if Teresa intended this miracle to happen and asked for it, her petition must have been granted. However, as a theologian and therefore aware of the implications and complications involved in this miraculous presence, he goes no further than to suggest that "in some manner", "somehow", Teresa may have been a living tabernacle.

To remain on safer ground, he goes on to state that, in any case, in her (as in every Christian in a state of grace) was verified the promise of our Lord: "If any man loves me and keeps my commandments, my Father will love him, and we shall come to him." It is not improbable that some preachers, carried away by their own eloquence, have already proclaimed as a fact this unproved assumption of a permanent presence in Teresa of the consecrated elements. Eloquence is not always controlled by reason! We should not be surprised, even, if some day Theresians put forward this suggestion of Pauline as a self-evident truth, needing no proofs, no demonstration. In such a way legends begin and grow.

In March 1896, the disease which had already followed a mild course for many months past declared itself dramatically. This is the time when Teresa was again given charge of the sacristy. The duties were not arduous and no employment could have given her more joy for, in handling the altar linen and the corporal, she saw herself, like the mother of Jesus, handling the garments of the Divine Child. She loved to see her face reflected in the Paten or Chalice as she prepared them for Mass. She would kiss the altar linen and even the large host which the priest was to consecrate at the altar. Lest sacristans in parish churches should feel inclined to imitate her example, we hasten to add that most parish priests would greatly object to this new form of devotion towards the Holy Eucharist, even if their sacristan was not, like Teresa, in an advanced stage of consumption.

V. THE "SUFFERINGS" OF TERESA

One need only read at random a chapter or two of *The Story of a Soul* to be struck by the insistence of St. Teresa on "her sufferings". She enjoys melancholy at six, and before she is ten, exclaims, "My God, Thou alone knowest what I have suffered", and at twelve, "she finds in suffering, charms that held her spellbound".

This continued throughout her life, and, two months before her death, as Teresa lay in bed in the infirmary, she heard that during the recreation one of the Sisters had said, "I do not know why they speak of Sister Teresa as if she were a saint. It is true that she has practised virtue, but hers was not one acquired through humiliation and suffering."[8] This seems to have roused Teresa, "To say that of me who suffered so much since my earliest infancy."[9] Another Sister the next day insisted, "They say that you have never suffered much." Teresa, pointing to a medicine glass full of a liquid bright red in colour, answered, "This is the image of my life. One would suppose it contained a delicious draught, in reality it is more bitter than anything I take. You think my life has been like a draught of delicious wine, but to me it has been full of bitterness."

Her emphatic and repeated assertions that her life was one of constant suffering are puzzling. No one in the convent was aware of it. Again, many saints have hard lives, but it is not usual to see them dwell so constantly and so feelingly on their tribulations. Could it be that Teresa's sufferings were due to her neurotic temperament?

Where are we to find the cause of these sufferings? Or rather, we might ask, of what did they consist? When did she suffer? At home Teresa was spoilt by her father, petted

---

[8] N.V., p. 96.
[9] There is in the French text an emphasis that we have tried to reproduce in the translation: "*Moi! qui ai souffert....*"

by her sisters. She had the easy life, the comforts, that could be expected in the French household of well-to-do people, and yet Teresa is always in tears. Père Ubald calls her a "weepy" child (*pleurnicheuse comme son père*). In Carmel, she no longer sheds tears as easily as at home, but she speaks of days of gloom, heavy trials, months of desolation, which she cannot explain. No one notices anything unusual. The Sisters think that she is being treated with special leniency,[10] and that by comparison with the others she is having an easy time.

This is very puzzling. What did Teresa mean when she was telling us about her "sufferings"?

She was not referring to the physical discomforts and hardships enforced by the Rule. There was no daintiness about the food or the way it was served. What of it? Hundreds of thousands of poor French people were not better fed than the nuns. It is true that, apart from a fire in the common-room, there was no heating in the convent and winter was an unpleasant season; but, after all, in the nineteenth century we have never known any institution, school or infant-school even, to be provided with any form of heating arrangements.[11] Carmelites rose at six in winter. This was not an early hour. In their schools, French boys always rose at five. Do not forget this was the life Teresa had deliberately chosen, and not for a minute can we assume that she lacked either courage or physical endurance, or that she was complaining.

Nor can we believe that when she spoke of her sufferings she was alluding principally to any marks of unkindness or of undeserved severity. It is true that she felt acutely the harshness of the Prioress, for, on the same page in which it is recorded, she exclaims that "suffering opened her arms wide to her". She also took to heart the mild hostility shown to her by some nuns, since, in a letter, she mentions "those pinpricks that gave her such pain". On the other hand we

---

[10] E, p. 150.
[11] This is no hearsay, but the experience of the author at school during the very years Teresa spent in Carmel.

are of opinion that even the public strictures of the Prioress on the inadequacies of Teresa and her slovenly floor sweeping were nothing out of the way. Any school boy or school girl of her age, still more any servant, would have had to face more strongly worded reproofs and would have thought nothing of it. The sharp pain they caused to Teresa was due to another cause: her abnormal and unnecessary sensitiveness. Again let us note, to her credit, how completely she overcame it. Her conquest of herself in this direction was remarkable. When she was twenty, and companion of novices, the acid and sub-acid remarks that the future nuns aimed at her did not seem to have even ruffled her composure in the slightest degree.

It is difficult to escape the conclusion that the sufferings of Teresa were mostly the outcome of a nervous temperament that made her react too intensely to situations which normal people would take in their stride. Like many people whose cerebral activity is over-developed and directed towards introspection, towards feelings, she had to pay for every day of exaltation by a corresponding mood of depression. These she could neither understand nor control, for she had no clue to their origin or meaning. This led her sometimes to think that it was the work of the devil. How often she had to endure those moods: "It is indeed a heavy cross when everything looks black.... In heaven nothing will look black."[12] Hence also those curious disturbances of the mind we observed in her "mysterious" illness, hence her scruples, her precocity, her responsiveness to sunshine or darkened skies, and other such peculiarities which mark her clearly as a neuropath.

What is very important, and yet does not seem to have attracted the notice it deserves, is that her struggles against this disability continued to the end of her life. As she had won the fight in 1886 against her propensity to tears, so she won it, up to a point, against her scruples in 1891 and, as we shall see later on, her last triumph was to be against a long

[12] E, p. 296.

protracted temptation of doubt.[13] One cannot be cured of one's temperament, because one cannot cease to be oneself, but it is possible to struggle against its manifestations.

The fight of Teresa against these disabilities is only a side issue in her total effort towards perfection, but such an important one that to pass it over in silence, as if it did not exist, is merely to obscure one of her glories. How rarely it is that "the victims of nerves", as they call themselves, manage to conquer them!

It is quite evident that the battle was never decisive, and went on endlessly. We have recorded Teresa's state of desolation during the retreat that preceded her Profession. This was not the end of her troubles. A fortnight later she was taking the *veil*. On this occasion she was "heavily *veiled* in sorrow", "she was not able to restrain her tears". The cause of her despondency was partly due to the absence of her father, then confined to a mental home, and that of the bishop, who had other engagements. Teresa adds that "for other reasons too it was a day of gloom".[14] She does not specify these reasons, but notes that, as usual, "her soul was profoundly at peace".

During the year that followed Teresa was subject "to all kinds of interior trials".[15] To her scruples was added a new fear. Not only was she, as usual, needlessly afraid of having offended God, but "she no longer knew whether God loved her". Take away the certainty of God's mercy and love and what remains to a saint? She was abnormally sensitive on this point. Here is an instance of it. She always wanted the sermons in a retreat to insist more on the mercy of God than on His justice. If it happened that a preacher spoke of sin and of God's punishments, or dwelt on the possibility for a nun of committing grave sins, this upset Teresa so seriously that she would grow pale, lose sleep and appetite and would

---

[13] N.V., p. 53, July 8th: "Once long ago she had taken too much pleasure in using some eau de Cologne which had been given her for travelling."

[14] E, p. 136.   [15] E, p. 138.

have become really unwell had the retreat lasted any longer. It was a kind of phobia with her and she needed reassurance all the time.[16]

She found it during a retreat in October 1891. For the second time since she had entered Carmel she met a priest to whom she was able to open her conscience. It was Père Alexis Prou, the preacher of the retreat. Previously she had always found it impossible to make clearly known what she called "her interior trials". This, by the way, is a characteristic of scrupulous people, who never explain their case because they themselves cannot understand it. He diagnosed the cause of her trouble. She was full of scruples, made unhappy by them, and what she needed was not to be convinced of God's justice, but of His love and mercy. "He launched her upon an ocean of confidence and love", and explained to her that her scruples were not sins and therefore could not offend God.[17] Surely she had heard this very often, but until then it had not come home to her as a personal message. This time it came as a revelation and she applied it to herself. But the way of scrupulous people towards a complete cure is a long one.

Two months later the advice of Mother Geneviève came at a time when she was again in one of her moods of motiveless depression. Teresa had a great veneration for this old nun, the foundress of the Carmel of Lisieux, who was then in the infirmary and very near death. When Teresa came to see her, Mother Geneviève, with her gift of observation, her experience and her common sense, saw at once the state of gloom in which the young Sister was floundering, and said to her pointedly: "Our God is a God of peace; serve Him in peace and joy."

Coming from one whom she looked upon as a saint, this timely exhortation comforted Teresa greatly, helped her to a better knowledge of herself and gave a new orientation to her life. After this episode, we cannot find any trace of those scruples which had been the bane of her religious life,

[16] Petitot, p. 187.   [17] E, p. 138.

although she was destined to undergo fresh mental trials later on.

There is now hardly any need for us to explain why it was that in the convent there was not one who suspected the ordeals which Teresa, under their eyes, in their midst, had undergone during those years of unbroken silence. Her "sufferings" were not physical. They were not visible or tangible, and Teresa, who considered that to ask for sympathy was an act of selfishness and weakness, spoke to no one about them during the nine years she spent in Carmel. It is only when, at the request of her superiors, she wrote the story of her life that these interior trials became known to others.

The Sisters around her could see the ready smile, the affability, the obedience. They were never told of the efforts which this perfection demanded. They said: "What praise does she deserve? That's the way she is, that's her nature. She could not do otherwise." Almost at the end of her life, when she was in the infirmary, one of the Sisters asked her whether she ever had had to fight against her natural inclinations. "I had a very troublesome nature," she answered. "It did not look like it, but I had to contend with it. I can assure you I have had to fight. . . ."[18]

In the two examples we are going to produce we shall find an illustration both of her continued nervous weakness and of the methods she used to overcome it. In one she accepts the situation and faces it out, in the other she runs away.

When she was acting as sacristan it was her duty to take back to the infirmary the keys of the Communion grating in the chapel. On one occasion she was doing this and was about to enter the ward because she wanted particularly to see a patient. Another Sister met her at the door. Treating Teresa as a junior, she explained "discreetly" that, lest the patient should be disturbed, she had better take the keys from her. "With all possible politeness," continues Teresa, "I told her that I was as anxious as she was that there should be no noise, adding that it was *my duty* to return them . . . and I

---

[18] *Summ.*, p. 430, Para. 1111-1113.

tried to enter the room. . . . The noise we made awoke the patient and the blame was cast upon me. The Sister made a lengthy discourse, the point of which being that I was the guilty person." Teresa did not argue. This little undignified scuffle for the possession of the tabernacle key had roused her temper to boiling point, and, fearing that if she stayed another moment she would lose it altogether, she sought safety in flight.

Then she continues: "My heart beat so violently that I could not go far and had to sit down on the stairs to taste in peace and quiet the fruits of my victory." Incidentally, the story is very well told. The "very gently", and "discreetly" and "all possible politeness" give us the full flavour of convent intercourse. This final incident will perhaps bring back to our mind a similar one that took place some years earlier, outside the door of Mother Prioress, when Teresa showed the same violence of feeling, gained over herself the same firm control and had also to stop on the stairs. Then, however, she had to cling to the banisters. Now it is enough to sit quietly on the steps and to wait for her agitation to calm down.

Here is the second incident, perhaps more characteristic still. In the chapel, she had a "fidgety" neighbour, whose rosary, clicking unendingly, irritated her to an extent she cannot describe. The effort she made to bear it with patience cost her so much that *she was bathed in perspiration*. And then, without knowing it, Teresa hit on the very device which persons suffering from nervous insomnia are asked to adopt when a clock or a rattling window is keeping them awake. Instead of getting annoyed, they are advised to listen to those noises. Presently they find they do not hear them any more and they go to sleep. "Instead of attempting vainly not to hear it, I set myself to listen carefully as though it was a delightful music and the time of my meditation was passed in offering this music to our Lord." Generally speaking, the senses of nervous people have an acuity which is more often a source of irritation than of pleasure to them. Teresa was well aware of this and she notes "that possibly she alone on account of her own very sensitive ear" had heard the devout fidget noisily counting her prayers.

She adopted the same rational method in the wash-house when a nearby Sister continually splashed her with dirty water, and with the same good results. "At the end of half an hour she had taken quite a fancy to this new kind of *Asperges*."

We cannot dismiss the subject without offering a word of explanation about the remarks that occur constantly, when Teresa is telling us of "her sufferings". At eleven and twelve, she speaks of the attraction of suffering and of its charms. When death was closing upon her, she declared, "I have found happiness and [even] joy on earth, but uniquely in suffering, for I have suffered much in the world."[19] What was the secret of this extraordinary joy? A very simple one; just this: what a joy it is to suffer for the one you love.[20] When suffering is useless we resent it as cruelty. Senseless, it bewilders us. Unjust, it drives us to revolt. If we know it can be turned to good purpose, we accept it willingly, and if we bear it for the sake of someone we love, we accept it joyfully.

Here is another feature of those spells of wretchedness she went through. Each time she is at pains to explain that she experiences a great peace of mind. In fact, when she talks of peace it is a sign she is going through a particularly severe crisis. In one and the same sentence she proclaims that on account of "spiritual aridity she found no comfort in heaven or on earth, *but nevertheless she was the happiest of mortals*".[21] At the end of her life she affirmed, "This inmost peace has been my portion for seven and a half years, never forsaking me amid the hardest trials."[22] On some occasions this peace seems a bit wintry and reminds us, perhaps, of the negligible difference there is between a cold war and a cold peace. But as she grew older this peace seems to have become

[19] N.V., p. 73.   [20] *Summ.*, Par. 2053.   [21] E, p. 131.
[22] E, p. 122.

more and more comforting in the measure that her surrender to God became more and more perfect. Absolute surrender banishes care about the present and about the future. Unquestioned obedience to God, in love and trust, relieved her of all cares, all fears, all responsibilities. It seems to us that this was the source of her astonishing peace.

She recognized, however, that it was easier to accept external trials, such as illness and bodily pain, than "*those insidious ones that come from within*", scruples and religious doubts.

VI. MY VOCATION IS LOVE

The word love can be found on every page of the autobiography: "My vocation is love." "In the heart of the church, I will be love." "I ask above all for love, love without stint." "Now I have no further desire, unless it be to love Jesus unto folly." "I wish to love till I die of love."

Love is one of those magic words that arrest the attention of men. It is also a word that seems to blind and blur their critical faculties. All this talk about love in *The Story of a Soul* has probably gained more admirers for St. Teresa than her real virtues; a most unreasonable estimate, for the sentimental love which they have in mind is not the one that made Teresa a saint.

We all agree that love alone makes a saint. But what kind of love? Teresa told Pauline about a "fiery dart of love", "transports of love", "assaults of love", which she experienced first at the age of fourteen and later on during her novitiate. Whatever these phenomena may be—for Teresa does not explain—they have no necessary connection with holiness. If they are mere sensations, internal perceptions, they can easily be misunderstood by the recipient, and in any case they cannot be verified, since they rest on his solitary word.

Nor do human virtues make a saint, nor hardship nor suffering, nor self-imposed penances, but only love for God and love of our neighbour for His sake. The teaching of the Gospel and the teaching of St. Paul meet clearly on this point: "I may give away all that I have, to feed the poor; I may give myself up to be burnt at the stake; if I lack charity [that is, love of God], it goes for nothing." And if we inquire further still and ask: how can we love God, since no man has ever seen Him, the answer is given us, clear-cut, beyond any possibility of misconception by the one they call the apostle of love, St. John. In his Gospel and in his epistles, he gives us an identical definition, "Love means keeping his commandments".[23] "The man who loves me is the man who keeps the commandments he has from me."[24] There is not much room here for sentimental love.

Unfortunately the style of Teresa, which is partly the expression of a very emotional temperament, partly a conventional manner of writing, tends to obscure the love-obedience, love-sacrifice, which was in her so real and so strong. Again and again she gives us the impression that she is hopelessly and incurably romantic; a sentimental young woman. Perhaps she was, but it is clear that most of the time her "love" was one of will and reason.

Any doubts about this can be dissipated by an attentive reading of the biography. Most of the time her state of mind is one of "aridity"—as she calls it—that is, a complete lack of sentimental satisfaction. Her language is emotional enough, but she feels nothing. Her meditation, her thanksgivings are most of the time a blank. She cannot concentrate. She goes to sleep. Her prayers are often full of distractions so that she is content to repeat the words of the Lord's Prayer and of the "Ave" with whatever attention she can summon. For years she is tormented by scruples, by the unreasonable and uncontrollable fear that she has committed some great sins, that God does not love her. There were times when her faith was clear and lively, when the thought of heaven was to her a source of delight, and times when it became a torment. She tried to live by faith, she willed to believe, but

[23] II John, 6.   [24] John XIV, 21.

she received no consolation. What did love mean to her in those difficult years? Surely not romantic feelings but action, obedience and the submission of a troubled spirit to the divine will. She found, in her scruples, her doubts, her days of gloom, the very means to prove her love for God.

It would, however, be a grievous error to think that this love of duty and resignation was all she knew, that the extravagant expressions she uses in and out of season are always pure rhetoric. That it was sometimes nothing more is evident. She wrote to a novice,[25] "Do not fear to tell Jesus that you love Him even though you may not actually feel this love." We have it from her that the poems she wrote during the last year of her life expressed not what she felt but what she wished to believe. For weeks and months she went without any "consolation".

Can any woman be entirely satisfied with a love of reason and will? Teresa's emotional nature craved for its transmutation into something less impersonal; hence those impassioned quotations from the *Song of Songs* (somewhat unexpected from a nun's pen) about "embraces of love", "a kiss from thy mouth", and so on. Most of the time these ardent appeals meant nothing more than her wish to love God, but there were occasions when this love became real, overwhelming, devouring as a flame. She ceased to be herself and she said, "I am love."[26]

We need not wonder at it! Love as a sentiment feeds and increases more on what one gives than on what one receives. Teresa gave everything she had, everything she was, to her divine Lover. On Him her mind dwells every minute of the day to the exclusion of all else. In her imagination she could hear, she could see Him, child, God-man. There were moments when His presence became so vivid, her perception of Him so overwhelming, that her feelings rose to raptures which she compares to fire and flames, to a burning furnace

---

[25] E, p. 196.
[26] N.V., pp. 51-2. "Oh what fire and what sweetness at the same time. . . ." etc.

or a glowing abyss. Such words seem as incoherent to us as the babblings of Peter and James after the Transfiguration, for the emotional ecstasies or sufferings of love, blinding lights as they are to the one who experiences them, remain a mystery, incommunicable, to those who only witness them. Such moments were exceptional and, save for one occasion, of short duration. The memory of these glimpses of heaven left behind them some intolerable longings, yet did not unfit her for her monotonous way of life. She knew clearly that such moments were not love, only the sweetness of love, that love for God is obedience, suffering, renunciation of self. This is the only way on earth. Emotional love is only an experience. It happens as a flood, a storm, or an earthquake, happens. It has little to do with will, choice, or reason. It is not what God wants from us. It adds nothing to our merits. "Love," wrote the great Teresa of Avila, "is serving God in justice, fortitude and humility." Teresa of Lisieux also said: "I have *laboured* to serve God." They were both very much in agreement.

VII. THE LITTLE WAY

Pauline, having been elected Prioress at the beginning of the year 1893, directed her sister to help Mother Marie de Gonzague, Mistress of Novices, in her task. The dethroned Prioress had never been a pleasant person to disagree with, and her wounded feelings at being put aside for Pauline were not going to make things easier for her young colleague. Teresa has been praised for her tact and prudence in avoiding scenes. This can only mean that scenes were at all times an unpleasant possibility.

Even though, in her new and undefined position, she cannot have been left much authority or initiative by her erratic partner, she acquitted herself of her task better than anyone else in Carmel could have done. She had, by advice and example, to train the novices in the Carmelite way of life, for what is sufficient for ordinary Christians in the world is not enough for contemplatives: these must have some acquaintance with ascetism and mystic theology.

The list of books on ascetism and mysticism by Catholic writers, from St. Gregory the Great to the nineteenth century, is a long and impressive one, and contains the names of many saints. St. Bernard, St. Bonaventure, St. Bridget, St. Teresa, St. Francis of Sales, Bossuet, and many others have written authoritative works on the subject. They do not make easy reading. No philosophical or theological books do, for, unless one reduces knowledge to a series of slogans, one cannot attain exactness as well as clarity, without method, divisions, distinctions which discourage most inquirers. Teresa had tried some of these books, and knew the *Imitation of Christ* (perhaps the simplest of them all) by heart. But, in general, while granting that these learned treatises were all admirable, she did not find any to her liking. She complained that they gave her a headache. "Sometimes when I read books in which perfection is put before us . . . my poor little head becomes dizzy. I close the learned treatise which tires my brain and dries up my heart. . . ."[27] Her emotional nature, which revelled in the poetry of St. John of the Cross, did not lend itself to a methodical and intricate approach to complicated problems. What could she do but devise a method of her own in teaching her novices the way to perfection? She seems to have thought it out principally during the last two years of her life, and, since our own experiences are the ones we know best and trust most, her system must have been the one which had answered her own needs.

Her life had always run on commonplace lines. When she was a child she had imagined herself going into battle by the side of Joan of Arc. In Carmel she could show her courage only by battling, broom in hand, with the spiders who had their home in the dark cupboard under the stairs. She had dreamt of facing proconsuls and kings and winning the palm of martyrdom In the convent she was required only to sweep the floors and clean pots and pans. She came to the

[27] Quoted by Mr. John Beevers in *Storm of Glory*.

conclusion that perfection could be acquired by very ordinary means, as well as by shining deeds, by very ordinary people as well as by learned, heroic, or miracle-working saints. Her teaching must be addressed to those "little souls" whose life was as uneventful as her own.

After having been the youngest at home, she found herself the youngest in the convent: hence, possibly, this childhood-complex we have already remarked upon. The designation she chose for her doctrine was: "The little way of spiritual childhood." In this respect she was thinking as much of the helplessness of the baby in arms, and its complete trust in its parents, as of the guilelessness and simplicity we attribute to children. At the same time it reminded her followers of the divine precept, "Unless you become like little children . . ."

At the end of her life this is how she formulated her doctrine in answer to her sister Pauline, who had asked what she meant by "her Little Way": "My Little Way is the way of spiritual childhood, the way of trust and absolute surrender."[28] At various times, she added explanations which made the meaning clearer. "This surrender," she said, "is a disposition of the heart that makes us humble and little in the arms of God, conscious of our weakness and trusting to the point of temerity in the kindness of our Father."

To sum up, her Little Way was for ordinary people. They could reach perfection by very ordinary means, because small acts of virtue are just as acceptable to God, and just as productive of merits, as great ones. Who, better than Teresa, knew the immense effort required to keep on all through the day the practice of little acts of self-mastery and self-denial that no one noticed or knew except God? This, she decided, was as good a material as any other with which to build up saintliness.

The foundation on which "the Little Way" rests is her deep realization of one's nothingness and helplessness, together with a complete trust in God's power and mercy. This

[28] E, p. 232, and N.V., p. 82.

resemblance to God, this deification of the soul which is the aim of Christian life, is beyond the natural powers of man. He cannot of himself deserve it, retain it or regain it, except God grants it as a gift.

This means both our own absolute helplessness and our absolute dependence on God. This means that humility and Hope are the virtues that will lead us to perfection.

Teresa called her teaching "an entirely new way". It seems difficult to call it new, and impossible to call it quite new. All the spiritual writers before her have taught that any kind of spiritual life rests on humility. In the Gospel there is a certain parable about a Pharisee that most of us remember. Before her no theologian had failed to recognize that Hope—that is, complete trust in God's power and love—was as essential as Faith or Charity. Again the Gospel is not completely silent on this important subject!

What was new was the arresting name of her doctrine: the way of spiritual childhood. What was new also was the odd comparison of the mechanical and unlovely contrivance called a "lift" with the loving arms of our Saviour; which will take us to heaven without any effort on our part just as an elevator takes travellers upward to their respective rooms.

She realized herself that this comparison had to be watered down and that God will not save us without our co-operation. A novice was so enthusiastic about this new doctrine that she told Teresa, "that she meant to preach it and to share it with her relatives and friends". The saint, with great sense and an understandable fear of uninformed zeal, answered: "Be very careful, it could be taken for Quietism." So it could. Teresa, who knew it, was constantly insisting, by teaching and example, on the necessity of good works as well.

Teresa attached an enormous importance to her "Little Way". Six weeks before she died she said: "I feel my mission is about to begin: my mission is . . . to give souls *My Little Way.*"[29]

[29] E, p. 231, and N.V., p. 81.

Père Petitot is certain that the Little Way has done much good in convents. It is doubtful, however, whether in the world outside convents it has—under that designation—received the attention and popularity Teresa had desired and expected. It is beyond question that, long before her time, the virtues of humility and Hope had been found necessary by every soul in search of God. Teresa's merit had been, by a new wording and by her insistence, to attract attention to some very ancient truths.

CHAPTER VI

THE LAST PHASE

I. THREE PROBLEMS

WE have now come to the last phase of Teresa's life, the eighteen months that preceded her death. It is a no less important period than the years which had gone before. Teresa, under the impact of illness, appears no different from what her self-portrait had revealed to us. On the contrary, the approach of death only accentuated these aspects of her character which we already know. The weakness of body and mind produced by a long illness too often uncovers the hidden flaws of one's nature. The patient becomes self-centred, querulous, inconsiderate, curiously confused in mind and unarmed against fear. Not so Teresa; her courage kept pace with her sufferings which, during the last six weeks, were almost unendurable. She never complained; she remained patient, considerate, and at all times accepted the circumstances of her coming death without wishing them different, seeing in them God's will.

We should know little of the last months spent in the convent infirmary if her sister Pauline had not kept a kind of journal, where she consigned not only her own impressions, but the course and progress of the illness, and preserved the sayings and discourses of her sister which she thought worth preserving.

As we read through these pages, perhaps with mixed feelings, some problems arise in our minds. They deserve our attention even though they do not supply us with all the evidence we need for full and satisfying answers.

The first is one of responsibility. In April 1896 it was evident that Teresa was seriously ill. She died eighteen months later. How was it that during twelve months nothing, or next to nothing, was done; that no treatment was given to check the progress of the tubercular condition that had manifested itself so very clearly? The Prioress was responsible for the welfare, bodily as well as spiritual, of the Sisters under her care. How are we to explain her inaction? Was her disposition towards Teresa one of tender affection, tempered by a higher spiritual charity, or was it one of malignant, though perhaps unconscious, hatred? We are not saying that either interpretation is correct or legitimate, but both have been strenuously maintained. Some will have it that Mother de Gonzague was the conscious instrument of God's will, while the novelist, M. van der Meersch, saw the situation as a dramatic duel, a cold war of silence between the saint, determined to keep silence and to put her superior in the wrong, and a Prioress no less determined to do nothing until Teresa came and said: I give in.

The second problem is this. During the last eighteen months of her life Teresa underwent a trial that, to the lay mind, seems as unexpected as it was incredible, for it happened to a saint: the tragedy of doubt. How could such a temptation overtake a saint and one sheltered in a convent? How far did these doubts go? Teresa's autobiography does not give us the full answer. The possibility that her life of sacrifice and love might end in utter nothingness did haunt her; we know that much. Did it go further still? This will remain for ever her secret! . . . "to write more might be to blaspheme . . . even now I may have said too much. May God forgive me!"[1]

Last of all, we cannot pretend that some of the statements attributed to Teresa during the last weeks of her illness are not startling. For she proclaimed her own sainthood with no uncertain voice, and she clearly anticipated her own canonization. For instance, some six weeks before her death, as the three sisters were standing round her bed, "suddenly fixing her eyes on us with a heavenly look, she said very distinctly:

[1] E, p. 157.

'You know very well that you are looking after a little saint.'" This declaration of one of her sisters, Marie, fits in with a number of others she made during the weeks that followed.[2] It is not usual for saints to announce their own canonization. In fact, we cannot recollect any instance of this kind of prophetic insight.

We do not pretend to hold the key to these puzzles. But this is no reason why we should pass by with averted eyes and pretend there is no problem at all. Still less could we dismiss them with unctuous and conventional considerations. At least we must state the difficulties as we see them and offer to the reader some suggestions that may enable him to make up his own mind.

II. THE RESPONSIBILITIES

On this question of the responsibility of Mother de Gonzague for serious lack of attention and medical care during the last illness of Teresa, we have already quoted M. van der Meersch. On the other side we shall now quote Père André Noché, S.J., who, in his book, *La réponse des textes et des archives*, takes the opposite view and completely exonerates the Prioress from negligence. His book is very well documented and produces all the facts, but at the end he side-tracks criticism by introducing a divine intervention, a kind of *deus ex machina* that turns the Prioress into a conscious instrument of Providence.

This easy process of interpreting history, which is used by many biographers of St. Teresa, from the day she was born until the day she died, is not one we care to follow. We shall give the facts as we find them and let the reader decide.

The first sign of tuberculosis was a soreness of the throat, not only painful but persistent, that started in June 1894. Four months later it was still receiving medical attention, and her throat was being cauterized with nitrate of silver. The

[2] Petitot, p. 117.

convent gossip related the trouble to the endless conversations of Teresa with her novices. We put this date on record to show that the sudden hæmorrhages of April 1896 were due to a long-standing condition and that when Teresa, one year later, tells Céline she will die this very year,[3] it means that already she was obscurely aware that all was not well with her. It is true that, in her biography, she states that in Lent the following year, 1896, she was perfectly well and in fact had never felt stronger in her life. But she was concealing the truth from herself as is the way with sick people, and specially with tuberculous subjects.

It was at the end of this very Lent that the warning came to her—this time unmistakable—that her condition was serious. After the long watch before the Altar of Repose on Holy Thursday night she had returned to her cell. Hardly had she laid her head on the pillow when she felt a hot stream rise to her lips and thought that death had come to claim her. "My heart," she says, "almost broke with joy. I had already put out the lamp, so I restrained my curiosity till morning and went peacefully to sleep." On rising at 5 a.m. she found her handkerchief drenched with blood. She was firmly convinced that this was the final call "heralding the coming of her Beloved", and she was glad.

These words of Teresa make the situation very clear. She knows her life is in danger, and her words about the "coming of her Beloved" can mean nothing else. She was so certain of it that, early in 1897, before she was officially acknowledged to be ill, she warned Céline that she expected to die in the course of the year. Our problem is this: how is it that for twelve months, from March 1896 to April 1897 she received no care, no treatment worth mentioning and was allowed to keep all the Rules without any relaxation? Must we blame the Prioress for neglect of duty, or Teresa for evasiveness, and almost for misrepresentation?

Knowing her condition, Teresa was bound by the Rule to

---

[3] Père Noché, C, p. 397, says: "Teresa remains convinced she will die very soon." See also C, p. 401.

disclose it to the Prioress, so that she might receive proper attention. According to the deposition of her sister Pauline this is actually what she said to Mother Marie de Gonzague. "This is what has happened to me, but please do not attach any importance to it: it is nothing. I am not in pain and will you please let me continue to follow the exercises of Holy Week."[4] The Prioress, this "woman of great sense" (*femme de tête*, as Père Noché calls her), agreed without any difficulty, and Teresa not only observed the rigorous fasting, and attended the long services of Good Friday, but, instead of resting, occupied the rest of the day with the arduous task of window-cleaning. While she was doing this, a novice passed by, and, horrified at the sight of her livid face and exhausted appearance, protested she would go and plead with Reverend Mother to have Teresa dispensed from continuing in this occupation. The saint would not allow it and went on with the work. That night for the second time she had another hæmorrhage. Did Teresa again inform the Prioress of this serious development or did she keep silence deliberately? We do not know. Her sister Pauline, summing up the whole of that year (April 1896 to April 1897), says: "For one year more [Sister Teresa] persuaded [the Prioress] so successfully not to attach any importance to her ailments, that as a result she was allowed to take part in all the devotional exercises and in the work of the community."[5]

Another Sister confirms this. "In spite of her illness she never exempted herself from devotions in common, nor failed to attend any of the public devotions, nor did she seek exemption from heavy tasks. She went on without complaining to the end of her strength. 'I can still go about,' she would say, 'I must stay at my post.'"[6] Père Noché, by inadvertence, seems to place in the spring of 1896 the energetic treatment (creosote, iodine, frictions, plasters, cuppings, red-hot needles, etc.) which was really given one year later.[7] The truth is that from April 1896 to the following April, apart perhaps from

[4] *Summ.*, p. 566, s. 1568. [5] *Summ.*, p. 566, s. 1570.
[6] *Summ.*, p. 430, s. 1115. [7] C, pp. 393, 394.

an occasional bottle of tonic wine and a meat diet for a short time, nothing was done.

We have on record an enigmatic remark of Teresa on this subject: As her own sister Pauline reproached her with having kept silence over her illness and the hæmorrhages of the year before, she said: "My poor little Mother, you must thank God I did not tell you, for, had you been aware of the state I was in and seen me so little cared for, it would have broken your heart." This sounds like a terrible accusation against some unnamed person. Père Noché explains at some length that this text does not imply that there was negligence or bad intention on the part of anyone, and that Teresa really considered herself '*trop bien soignée*'. Maybe! But why did she not say so more clearly? Could it be that once more her dramatic way of speaking is leading the reader astray?

Anyway, for twelve months no treatment worth mentioning was given although a very troublesome cough persisted. Dr. de Cornières, who attended the convent, seems to have been completely unaware of the nature of her complaint. Otherwise, instead of prescribing a bottle of tonic, he might have realized that daily fasting and hard work were not the right treatment for tuberculosis. He might even have suggested the fresh-air cure which was already well known in France. Perhaps he did, and perhaps the Prioress ruled it out on the grounds that it was not proper for nuns to keep their windows open at night.[8] Perhaps, again, he may not have heard of the hæmorrhages of April, for Teresa, who had been so reticent with the Prioress, may have been equally reserved with the doctor.

It is idle to pretend that signs of improvement could be

[8] This is the excuse that was given as late as 1903 in a convent of Ursulines (as the author has every reason to know) in a case parallel to that of Teresa. As for the fresh-air cure in 1897, the author remembers a fellow student of his, named Camenen, who was suffering from tuberculosis. In obedience to doctor's orders, he kept his window open day and night, a procedure that caused much interested comment amongst us. The date has some bearing on the subject: he died in the summer of 1897.

seen, and that the Prioress was justified in letting Teresa continue work, fasting, exercises, as if she had been in good health. There were short apparent respites and that was all. In September 1896, she was clearly worse. Most nights she was kept awake by violent fits of coughing, and sat up in bed in order to be able to breathe. At five or six in the morning she would get up and go down to the chapel with the others. On one occasion, after she had been given a strong plaster of belladonna or mustard, she went to Mass and Communion as usual and Pauline, anxious about her, followed her up to her cell afterwards. There she found her sister completely exhausted, sitting on a little low stool and leaning against the wooden partition. She reproached her for her imprudence, and Teresa replied: "This is not too much suffering for the privilege of Holy Communion." Her cell was isolated, and she told Pauline she would rather stay there than go down to the infirmary, "because here," she said, "I disturb no one, and they do not hear my coughing." It has been affirmed repeatedly by the Sisters that before April 1897 no one noticed that there was anything amiss with Teresa: "nothing abnormal". "She was not ill."[9] This seems curious, but may be possible. Much depends, of course, on what one means by "ill". Teresa, we must agree, could still stand on her feet, but in a medical sense she was ill and already doomed and there was somebody in the convent who should have known it. That was the Prioress.

It is in this deplorable condition that throughout the winter she went on keeping the hard rules of Carmel. Up at six, prayers, office, Mass in the cold chapel, then work until dinner at eleven. The hours of the afternoon were also divided in the same way between work and prayer, and the day ended in the chapel with Matins and spiritual reading from 9 p.m. to 10.15 p.m. After this they could at last retire to their cold cells for rest. Once, a young infirmarian, Sister Marie de la Trinité, who could see for herself that Teresa, through her silence and her obedience to the Rule, was hasten-

[9] C, p. 397 and note 38.

ing her death, went to see the Prioress to obtain for her a dispensation from attending Matins at 9 p.m. The woman answered roughly: "I have never heard before of such young people as this who think of nothing but their health. In former times one would never have thought of missing Matins. If Sister Teresa of the Child Jesus has come to the end of her strength, let her come and tell me so herself." "No fear," adds Sister Marie de la Trinité, "Teresa was not the one to go and complain."[10]

Teresa gave the Prioress some sort of account of her health because it was her duty to do so, but it seems that she minimized the gravity of her state, and merely said that she coughed, which everyone could hear, and that she was tired, which everybody could see, adding that she felt quite able to go on following the Rule.

"Our Mother knows very well that I am *tired*: it is my duty to tell her what I feel, and since in spite of it she gives me permission to keep step with the community, it must be that she is inspired by God, who wants to grant my wish to go on working to the very end." And she would shake off her fatigue, saying: "If I die, I die."[11]

She was not to die just yet. The human body—in the young at least—possess incredible reserves of strength on which one can draw as long as courage keeps up. Teresa held on until the end of the winter, when at last her strength, not her courage, gave way. One night, as she was going up the stairs leading to her cell, she found that she had to rest and sit on every step for breath, and it took half an hour for her to reach her room, one hour more to take off her garments, with long pauses between each. She knew then that her wish to go on working to the end would not be granted and she told Sister de la Trinité, who warned the Prioress and Pauline of what had happened. From then on, there was no neglect and all the futile and sometimes cruel medications of those days came into play. By the end of June it was evident that her death was a matter of time, a short time.

[10] C, p. 398.   [11] *Summ.*, pp. 714, 513.

The Prioress from this moment did all that was in her power for the patient, and allowed Sister Geneviève (Céline) and Mother Agnès (Pauline) to nurse her. As for Sister Marie du Sacré Cœur (Marie), she was allowed to see Teresa freely and to attend to the preparation of her food. These concessions do not strike us as acts of staggering generosity, but Père Noché describes them as being "absolutely exceptional", "very generous and liberal measures".[12] In favour of the Prioress, let us also add that on various occasions she expressed her admiration for Teresa, whom she called the Angel of the Community, praised her to everybody and was even observed to break down and weep without restraint in the chapel while prayers were being offered for her recovery.

There are, however, two occasions when, maybe, she does not appear in a very favourable light. Some five weeks before the end came, on the 22nd day of August, Teresa was seized with intense pain in the intestines. A doctor should have attended to this new complication, but the Prioress did not wire to Dr. la Nèele until the 30th. Pauline, in her diary, marks the strong disapproval she felt by noting that during the absence of Dr. de Cornières on holiday during August, "Mother Prioress only allowed Dr. la Nèele to make three visits although he declared that she should be seen by a doctor every day." In September, Dr. de Cornières recommended hypodermic injections of morphia, "but the Prioress would not allow them, and Teresa was only given some syrup of morphia and then very little and very rarely, for the Prioress also objected to this sedative". These two entries, in their studied moderation, express Pauline's clear disagreement with Mother Prioress, who probably thought it was shameful for a Carmelite to be given relief by this method.

The attitude of Mother Marie de Gonzague during the illness of Teresa has been variously interpreted. M. van der Meersch sees in it a deliberate persecution. He calls her a Cain, and a torturer. He speaks of unconscious ferocity, of furious hatred, of a diabolical gift for deceiving herself. These

[12] C, pp. 405, 406.

expressions are evident exaggerations, which no artistic intentions can justify. But were they no more than exaggerations?

When we were dealing with the treatment meted out to Teresa, as postulant and novice, by the Prioress,[13] we endeavoured to keep an even balance and produced all the excuses that could be pleaded in her favour. We have not pretended (as some Theresians have done) that she was a new Ignatius of Loyola, using harshness and humiliations towards Teresa uniquely for her highest good and as an effect of her Christian love for her.

On the other hand it seems to us that all the expressions of gratitude and devotion used by Teresa towards her persecutor sound too exaggerated to be true.[14] They prove little except that saints can turn everything to their spiritual advantage, that she was speaking as a saint and that she practised what she had preached to the novices: "where one finds an evident defect, hasten to look for virtues and good motives . . . what appears to be a fault may very well be an act of virtue."[15]

If we turn now to the complete and astonishing neglect of the serious condition of Teresa for a whole year, surely a lot of explaining is needed. The Prioress knew of these hæmorrhages of the lung, and whatever Père Noché may say, this, in 1896, was taken as a very sinister symptom, deserving serious attention. In the *Epilogue* of the biography we are given the glib explanation that "Reverend Mother was blind to the real state of things". She had no right to be. The community was a small one; the nuns were entirely under her care, and she was in daily contact with them all. They were her responsibility and nobody else's. Why did she not do anything? Had she no common sense, no eyes? Or had she no feelings and no pity?

---

[13] Chap. IV, Sect. I.
[14] On one occasion when the Prioress was ill, Teresa states that "Jesus is very desirous to enjoy in heaven the presence of our darling mother. . . ." (see p. 19). This is an example both of this exaggeration, and of an amusing lack of a sense of humour.
[15] E, p. 163.

Let us concede, however, that Teresa did not enlighten her very much, and the reason is that she had made up her mind that she would follow the community exercises up to her death. She thought she could manage it, by sheer will power, as she had managed to enter Carmel at fifteen, and she went on repeating that "God does not inspire wishes that are incapable of fulfilment".[16] This time, however, her body was going to fail her, and she was not allowed to have her wish.

This same panegyrist absolves the Prioress altogether by stating that " she regulated herself on what Teresa said; Teresa regulated herself on the divine inspiration she received, and neither of them paid any attention to Sister Marie de la Trinité".[17] This silence, he says, was the result of "obedience to a clear inspiration of God's grace". Here we must part company. It is too easy, each time a difficulty occurs, to explain it by an act of God, and say "nobody's fault". God can make use of our blunders, even of our sins, but we must not make him directly responsible for them. They are *our* blunders, *our* sins. The Prioress cannot evade all responsibility by casting the blame on Teresa: "This is what she said, I acted on it." It would almost amount to saying that Teresa committed suicide.

For we cannot altogether absolve Teresa of imprudence. Can we invoke divine inspiration? To her novices she said: "When you are ill, tell Mother Prioress." "Then, whether anything is done or left undone, put yourself in the hands of God and do not worry. In telling Reverend Mother you have done your duty; the rest is not your concern, it is God's concern." This may be an excellent rule for small ailments, and for people who are always thinking of their health, but, after all, even Reverend Mothers are liable to make mistakes, to forget, and the above rule, if the ailment happened to be a serious one, might be very unfair not only to the patient but to the superior. This is, however, the rule Teresa followed

[16] C, p. 399 and N.V., *passim.*
[17] E, pp. 399, 400.

in the course of her illness. The intention was admirable, but was it a prudent rule? Was it a fair rule?

Did she consult her confessor quite candidly, or did she judge, as she did ten years earlier that "she did not feel the need of any other guide but Jesus"?[18] We do not know, but it is likely that, had she done so, His advice would have been: "Your health is not your property, it is the means of serving God. You must take reasonable care of your body."

In misleading the Prioress by her silence and her insistence that she was able to continue working, she was doing her an injustice. She exposed her to the grave accusation of neglecting her duty towards the sick. In fact that is what happened and to this day we are left wondering whether strong dislike —M. van der Meersch said, diabolical hatred—dictated the conduct of the Prioress towards Teresa, and made her, in part at least, responsible for her death.

We have given the facts. We do not feel competent to offer a final solution. We think that Mother Marie de Gonzague was an emotional and mentally unstable woman, guided by her likes and dislikes, unfair and at times unjust; and yet we believe that she retained, in spite of it all, a wish to be just, to do her duty, to be faithful to her vocation. Such contradictions are not so rare as one thinks, and we do not believe that she was deliberately cruel to Teresa. A time came when she felt a great respect for the strength of character, the clear mind, and the evident perfection of the religious life of the young saint. It is possible that she deceived herself into believing that her treatment of Teresa was inspired by a pure sentiment of duty. All the same, there lingers in our mind a suspicion that had Teresa been one of her favourites she would have treated her differently; and then again, perhaps we are wrong!

III. THE TORMENT OF DOUBT

Physical pain is hard enough to bear; mental pain can be a

[18] E, pp. 92, 125.

worse torment. She was a saint, and was fully conscious of it, as we shall see presently; and yet "the thought of her approaching death was robbed of all feeling of happiness". "Her soul was enveloped in thick darkness." The life to come, Heaven, the invisible world of angels and blessed spirits had ceased to have for her the warm reality of living things and their nearness. They had become cold intellectual concepts that gave her no joy, no comfort. Her divine Friend had gone far away, it seemed, or at least kept an unbroken silence. She did not doubt; she knew she was not forsaken, but *she felt* like one unloved and rejected. For more than one year, almost from that day when, at the thought of approaching death, "she had knelt at the feet of the Prioress to confide her happiness to her", she had been haunted by the fear of doubt. Her soul dwelt in darkness or, as she says more accurately still, in a land of fog. In a fog we no longer *see* the people, the houses, the sun. We know they are there, but we feel lost.

We cannot do better than use her own words to describe her bewilderment and horror at this—to her—novel situation. "Of a sudden, the fog that surrounds me finds its way into my very soul and so blinds me that I can no longer see the lovely pictures of my promised home . . . it has all faded away." "When my heart . . . tries to find rest and strength in the thought of an everlasting life to come, my anguish only increases. . . . A voice cries mockingly: You dream of light and fragrance, you believe that the Creator of these wonders will be for ever yours. Hope on. . . . Look forward to death! It will give you not what you hope for, but a night darker still, the night of utter nothingness!"[19] "To write more might be a blasphemy . . . even now I may have said too much. May God forgive me!"

"You may think I have exaggerated. If one judged by the poems I have composed this year, it might seem that I have been inundated with consolation, that I am a child for whom the veil of Faith has been almost rent asunder . . . but it is

[19] E, pp. 156, 157.

not a veil . . . it is a wall which reaches to the very heavens, shutting out the starry sky." "When I sing in my poems of the happiness of heaven and of the eternal possession of God I feel no joy, I sing only of *what I wish to believe.*"

In this page we seem to discover a new Teresa. How intensely she feels, how intensely she writes! Too often in her biography she loses herself in a maze of sentiment and uses a language of convention which makes it difficult to disentangle what is really hers and what is a mere echo of convent speech. Here she speaks as she feels. She cries out her anguish, her fear, as would a child lost in a forest. This is real, this is true, and our heart goes out to her, because we discover that at times she was, after all, somewhat like us.

Our first impression is one of stupefaction. Can a saint feel like this? Were these doubts a real temptation to Teresa? Were they really doubts? How did they come to her? We shall try to answer these and kindred questions in the clearest way we can, and must ask the reader for some patience if we have to be somewhat technical.

We should have, first of all, some idea of what is meant by faith if we are to understand what is meant by doubt. Faith, in a Catholic sense, is not just an opinion, a probability, a sentiment. It is an unshakable conviction that God has spoken to man, that His word is true and that it comes to us through the voice of the Church.

Faith is a gift, a free gift of God. By our prayers we can obtain it; but strictly speaking we cannot deserve it. It is a gift that we are free to accept or reject, that, having once possessed, we can lose, for the gift of God is not forced upon us and the choice remains always open to us. It is because they are free that saints are praised for the firmness of their faith and unbelievers condemned for refusing the gift of God or for throwing it away. Because they accept or reject it freely they are responsible.

If faith were against reason, how could this be? Pascal once pointed out that in matters of faith the light is not all on one side, nor is the obscurity; the evidence on either side is not so overwhelming as to compel our assent. The scales seem fairly evenly poised until our free decision makes them rise or fall this way or that. In our best moments, when unselfishness, pity, sacrifice, love of truth fill our hearts, we find it easy to believe. When our lives run on selfish and material lines, on money, pleasure and success, spiritual things cease to appeal to us and sink below the horizon.

Bearing in mind these explanations, and some of the comments of Teresa herself, it becomes clear that she never lost her faith; that, in fact, there was no real danger of her losing it. It was a trial, rather than a temptation, a fear of doubt, more than a real doubt. With all her heart she wished to believe, for she would have prayed and suffered and lived in vain if there was nothing beyond the grave. With all the power of her will she chose faith and she prayed for faith. "I have made more acts of faith," she wrote, "during the past year than in all the rest of my life." And three weeks before her death she told her sister Pauline: "How I have been tempted during this night. But I never ceased making acts of faith."

Her "doubts" were not of an intellectual nature. She was not a philosopher, like St. Thomas Aquinas, and books of arguments against the possibility of survival did not come her way. The neglect of spiritual duties, the moral failures which are the most frequent cause of loss of faith among people in the world, had no place in her life. These distressing doubts seem to us to have been partly due to a failure of the imagination, which is necessarily baffled by the concept of an invisible world. Most of us find useful such symbols, such substitutes for reality, as the pictures of Fra Angelico, with a heaven full of very human-looking angels in brilliantly coloured robes. Discard the symbols, and our senses fail us. There remains only some notions as abstract as those of an infinite space or an endless time.

We said "partly due to a failure of imagination" because we must look at her nervous temperament as a contributory, if not a principal, cause. We must remember those years of scruples she went through before entering the convent and even afterwards. The essence of scruples is that they are senseless and for this reason cannot be dealt with by argument. The sufferer is not open to logic or common sense. He is confused, uncertain, yet obstinate; his trouble is pathological, not intellectual. The same can be said of the kind of "doubts" which troubled Teresa. No argument would have been of any avail. She could not have said why she doubted that which had seemed so clear before. She could not assign any particular reason for it. "I wish I could explain what I feel, but it is beyond my power," she said.[20] As in the past she had been tormented by the baseless fear of having offended God, knowing it to be baseless, so now she was tormented by fear of unbelief just as senseless as her scruples.

IV. "I AM A SAINT"

The third problem is not one of which we can dispose in a few words, nor one which one could prudently consider in the abstract, and apart from the circumstances in which it arose. The pronouncements of Teresa about the supreme importance of her autobiography, her future glory on earth and her future tasks in heaven, as well as her quasi-announcements of her coming canonization, belong, all of them bar one, to the last few weeks of her life.[21] She was then lying in the infirmary, in weakness of body and in anguish of soul, wondering at one moment whether her lucidity of mind was giving way,[22] at another, speaking of the evil spirits that were tormenting her, and of the need of prayers in which she stood, and then telling her sisters, "You know very well that I am a little saint."[23] There is here a problem that insists on our attention. Père Petitot has suggested a solution which we accept as far as it goes, but it does not seem to us to go far enough and does not entirely resolve the difficulties.

---

[20] E, p. 155.
[21] "I will spend my Heaven in doing good upon earth."
[22] N.V., p. 144.   [23] Petitot, p. 117.

During May and June, Teresa was already very ill. She chose, however, to continue in her little cell, because, she explained, there at night her cough would not disturb anyone as she had no neighbours. At the beginning of July, the Sisters believed her to be in imminent danger and there was some talk of the last sacraments. In any case they judged it necessary to have her taken down to the infirmary where she would be under constant supervision and would receive proper attention. Her three sisters, Marie, Pauline and Céline, received permission to see her as often as their duties allowed it. This must have been a great comfort for Teresa. Marie's special task was the preparation of her food; that of Pauline—always her favourite sister—was the more general one of acting as companion and spiritual guide. Teresa, now weak and helpless, depended more than ever on her masterful, obstinate, clever, Pauline.

For the first time since Teresa had left her home, a new intimacy began and grew between them. We have not forgotten that, during her first five years in Carmel, Teresa had kept her "little mother" at arm's length and only spoken to her as she would have done to any one of the Sisters in the convent. During the years that followed, her silence had, up to a point, continued. Prior to April 1897 she did not keep Pauline informed of her hæmorrhages, nor of the progress of the disease, nor even of the scanty care and attention she received. In the infirmary there could be no longer any question of keeping Pauline at a distance and they found themselves in the same old relationship as in the distant days when, at home, Pauline was her "little mother", and Teresa the baby of the family.

It was Pauline who, day by day, made notes of everything that happened at the infirmary during the last five months, from May to September. To her we owe practically all the knowledge we possess of this last phase. A small selection of her notes has been condensed into a booklet called *The Last Words, Novissima Verba*, and they are an important source of information.

In the notes of Pauline, all is not of equal value. Some of the entries may have seemed precious to her, because, in a family, the most insignificant sayings of a dying person are preserved and treasured at least for a time. To us, it seems that not a few of them were not worth recording. She is given some violets and says, " Ah, the scent of violets! " And that is the whole entry. This kind of remark does not add to our knowledge of St. Teresa and seems to us meaningless. Some entries are childish. These, however, have the advantage of throwing a light on the character of the saint.

"When they give me milk and rum I offer it to St. Joseph and say to myself, 'Oh, this will do poor St. Joseph a lot of good!'"

Let us say, however, by far the largest number of entries add much to what we already knew of Teresa, and some of them are of very great value, as we shall see in the course of this chapter.

It is not Teresa alone who is portrayed in these pages with her courage, her resolute, almost eager acceptance of pain, but the whole convent as well. We are given a good picture of this little community of nuns, for, one by one, they all come to her bedside with their endless questions, foolish or sensible, often gruesome, tactless nearly always, and, it seems to us, showing more curiosity than sympathy. Had not Teresa herself said, "Saints who suffer never excite my pity."[24] They all come: one in a combative mood, another tearful, and a third, who had nothing to say, gaped and grinned nervously at the foot of the bed. Poor Teresa! Exhausted as she was, she found the company of the one who moaned and of the one who laughed equally irritating and said so. Once, after being plied endlessly with questions, she complained: "They worry me with their questions. I might be Joan of Arc before her judges."

Some of Teresa's visitors discussed, before her and with her, sickness and death and all attending circumstances with a lack of reticence which, to us in England, sounds almost ghoulish.

[24] E, p. 314.

One point attracts their attention specially: "Are you frightened of death? Would you be frightened if you were told now that you are going to die this minute?" Teresa remarked, when they had gone: "They tell me I shall be frightened." In front of her, some of the nuns talk of the pitiful distortions of the face which occur generally at the moment of death[25] and Teresa retorts that, if this happens to her, anyway she will smile afterwards. On July 30th they thought the end was near and they brought down the straw mattress on which it was the custom to lay the bodies of the dead. They did not trouble to hide it out of sight and, by the open door, Teresa saw it in the passage. "Here is our mattress," she said, "ready for my corpse." The Sisters did not mean any unkindness and we should be much mistaken if we thought Teresa was upset in any way. It is in the same matter-of-fact spirit that we shall see her calmly admiring the flowers they have sent for her funeral.

On occasion they tried to cheer her up. We must concede that their unintelligent but well-meant efforts were not always well received. A novice had brought her a book with pictures and stories, hoping it would be a change and a distraction. Teresa refused it: "How could you think that I would be interested?" Another day, a visitor, hoping to please her, related a conversation between the Prioress and some Sisters who had discussed "her past beauty and charming appearance". At this time, almost exactly one month before her death, Teresa's face had the unhealthy puffiness one notices in some patients, but otherwise her body was a mere skeleton. She answered almost petulantly: "Ah, what is that to me! It does not interest me, it bores me. When one is near death one cannot take pleasure in such thoughts."[26] It is clear, even when it is not expressly stated, that most of the conversations of Teresa with the nuns (we are not including her sisters) were a faithful echo of the tittle-tattle of the recreation hour. What else was there, after all, that could be of interest to talk about? Judging by the questions they ask in the infirmary,

[25] N.V., p. 59.   [26] N.V., pp. 165, 178.

there were two great topics of interest. The first related to the course of Teresa's illness, her chances of recovery and her reactions when she knows she is going to die. The second concerned these new reports that were circulated among them that Teresa is a saint. Two controversial subjects, for there is no agreement among the nuns on these points. How did the second rumour originate? Who started it? Was it Pauline? We do not know. But we find the good Sisters coming again and again to the infirmary and trying to elicit from Teresa the answers that will help them to make up their minds on these points, and to report them to the community. Will you be frightened? Are you a saint? they inquire. For a long time they could not decide whether or not Teresa was as seriously ill as they had been told. Teresa herself, influenced by their insinuations, began to wonder, against all evidence, whether, after all, she was going to recover. "Then perhaps the Sisters will look upon me as a fraud." Sometimes she says, "If I get better . . ." and she does not rule out the possibility of going out one day to Indo-China. These speculations came to an end some time in July when the rapid progress of the disease made it evident there could be no recovery.

Repeatedly the talks turned on her reputed sanctity, either by implication or quite openly. But we must not rule out the great probability that there were some heated differences of opinion on the subject. Not all the nuns thought her a saint. Not all of them even were fond of her. We have already alluded to those gossips, under her window, who asked each other in earnest what one could find and say in the obituary circular of Teresa since she had never done anything worth recording. Again another Sister, who had brought Teresa some meat extract, felt personally offended when she refused it and told someone, "I cannot see why they talk so much about Sister Teresa. She has never done anything worth mentioning. One cannot even call her a good religious."[27] We have also reported that occasionally her sanctity had been questioned by the community on the grounds that she had had

[27] *Summ.*, p. 1001, s. 2863, quoted by A. Noché.

THE LAST PHASE

an easy time and had never suffered. It did not take long for an obliging Sister to go to the infirmary and repeat this piece of gossip to Teresa, who seems for once to have been put out by this untrue report. We know that, at one time, there had been a nun who had been jealous of Teresa and never missed an opportunity to make herself unpleasant. We may, perhaps, assume that she relented when Teresa became ill. In any case she is not mentioned among the infirmary visitors. There is, however, another one, of whom we hear very little, who later on declared that the piety of Teresa seemed to her "childish and superficial". It is not safe to disagree with the majority, even with a pious majority, and this good nun who, as we have every right to suppose, led in the convent a life of poverty, chastity, obedience, and prayer, was denounced by the others as "a compound of rationalism and human views. She was well known in the convent for her lack of supernatural sense."[28] It seems a bit hard on her to have been dubbed a rationalist in nun's clothing because of a difference of opinion. A warning and portent of the fate of those who, in any community, refuse to join the chorus!

How very embarrassing it must be for a saint to be asked for a declaration of her own saintliness or even merely to have the point discussed in front of her! She probably knew the story of St. Philip Neri being sent to a convent in order to investigate a case of reputed holiness. The nun was called to the parlour and straight away St. Philip asked her, "Are you the saint?" The nun modestly answered, "Yes, Father." Thereupon, St. Philip decided he knew all he needed and told the holy nun she could go. The examination was over. More sensible than this nun, Teresa replied, "I am not a saint. All you see in me is God's gift and God's work." A leading question was put to her. "Considering that so many saints have been afraid of God's judgments, afraid of being among the lost, how is it that you are not afraid?"[29] Since no man can be sure of his salvation, there seemed to be no possible answer to this very pertinent question. Teresa took refuge in

[28] Petitot, p. 94.   [29] N.V., p. 58.

her favourite phantasy. She was still a little baby. "For little children," she said, "there is no eternal punishment!"

We have by now obtained a general impression of the atmosphere of this sick room where the visitors' conversations ran mostly on sickness and death and, with some of them, on the probability that Teresa was a saint.

To complete the picture we must now bring into it her sisters who, unlike the passing visitors, stayed with her most of the time, Pauline especially. For the first time in eight years these two spoke to each other without restraint, without reserves, as they felt. In the weakness induced by pain and helplessness, Teresa opened her heart to her sister without any inhibitions. That the conversation was a good deal about herself was very natural on the part of Pauline because she was devoted to her younger sister, or on the part of Teresa because sharp physical suffering forced her to retire within herself. What could be more natural also than speaking about the inevitable ending, death, and the times that would follow, and then just as inevitably of the future glory to come? It is clear that as Teresa had long ago decided that to become a great saint was to be her life purpose, so also Pauline, for some years past, had made up her mind that Teresa *was* a saint. We might go further. When, as a Prioress, she bade her sister write her autobiography, a very unusual request to make to a young nun, only twenty-one years old—had she already some suspicion that canonization was a possibility not to be ruled out? Had this vague surmise become clearer when, in 1897, she begged Mother de Gonzague—again a Prioress—to order Teresa, already on the brink of death, to continue and complete her task? She seems to have had some more definite hopes still when, during the last weeks of her sister's illness, she was taking notes daily for future reference, and by her leading questions eliciting materials for her purpose. All the time she was making suggestions to Teresa about the manner of her death and about her future glory. On August 9th she was telling her quite openly that "*the day would come* when they would praise her virtues". Although

Teresa answered that it is God alone that should be praised, it seems that the same idea had already crossed her own mind. Five weeks earlier, she had said, perhaps without attaching any importance to it: "In heaven it would please me so much if you wrote a pretty poem in my honour, for it seems to me that the saints are pleased when you sing their praise."[30]

Teresa had finished the story of her life at the beginning of July. Until then she had not seemed to attach any importance to it. In the pages written for the Prioress she had said: "I do not even ask of what use this manuscript could be and should you burn it before my eyes, without having read it, I should not be in the least distressed." We must assume that she meant what she said, but under the influence of Pauline she changed her mind very quickly. A few days later, on the 11th July, Pauline was "conversing with her about her manuscript and the great profit that would accrue to souls". Teresa answers, "Yes, but they will see that everything [*I am or have done*] comes from God. The glory that will come to me (from its publication) will be a gift from above, it will not be my own." A week later they are still talking about the manuscript and she is preoccupied with the necessity of revision—for she has now resolved to have it published—and she tells Pauline, on July 16th, "you must revise everything I have written. If you think it fit, leave out some things or add others that I have explained to you in conversation; it will be the same as if I was doing it myself. Remember this and have no scruples on this score." She had this publication in view when she specified that in her manuscript she has said practically nothing about the divine justice, but Pauline will find her mind on this matter in a letter addressed to Fr. Roulland.[31] "My sister," said Pauline, "knowing that she had discovered a priceless treasure, wanted to make it known to the world." It is clear that, under Pauline's guidance, she has decided that her story must be published, and her sister must correct, complete, and edit the

[30] N.V., p. 39.   [31] N.V., pp. 80-1.

manuscript. A fortnight later they are still discussing the matter, and this time she underlines "*the supreme importance of her work*". "Mother, after my death you must not tell anyone about my manuscript until it has been published. Otherwise the devil will lay more than one snare to prevent and spoil God's work." A few days later, after reading again at the request of Pauline a passage which her sister judged incomplete, her eyes filled with tears. "I asked her why she wept, and she explained with angelic simplicity: 'What I read here is so much myself. . . . Mother, these pages will do so much good. . . .' In inspired accents she added, 'Ah, I know it so well, *everybody will love me.* . . .'" (The italics are Pauline's.) We are not going to elaborate. Read these texts carefully and draw your own conclusions. Some have said Teresa was inspired. We agree; but the next question is: where did the inspiration come from? On this occasion the answer is: Pauline.

They knew Teresa's predilection for the poetical works of St. John of the Cross and quoted and applied to her some passages of his works. Someone—which of the three sisters was it?—perhaps to encourage Teresa to speak of her own perfections quoted: "The souls that have reached the perfection of love can, without danger, contemplate their own supernatural beauty." The implication was, of course, that Teresa had reached perfection. "What beauty?" said Teresa. "I cannot at all see my beauty. I can only see the grace of God." Five days later Pauline returned to the subject and quoted the words of St. John of the Cross. "They die in the midst of admirable transports and the raptured onslaughts of love."[32] This was too much for the sense of reality of Teresa, who, just then, was more acutely aware of her physical sufferings than of transports of love, and she sighed: "Transports, joy and transports! (*If you mention this to others*) you will have to explain they are only to be found right at the bottom of my soul." To die of love! Pauline, or someone else, had already broached the subject to Teresa whose comment (on

[32] N.V., pp. 139-40.

July 4th) had been: "To die of love (*that is for the sake of someone*) is not the same thing as dying in transports (*of love*)."[33] But Pauline, who did not lack tenacity of purpose, reopened the subject in August and, as we shall see, introduced it boldly in the accounts she gave of her sister's death.

Pauline was hoping that her sister had special premonitions, some kind of revelation about the future, and she said: "Have you any intuitions about the date of your death?" Teresa took it up—as it was intended she should—in the sense of special knowledge given her directly from above, and her answer should be weighed with care: "Ah, Mother," she said, "intuitions! If you knew how destitute I am [of such things]. I do not know any more than you do. *I guess nothing except through what I hear and feel.* Yet in my soul in the midst of darkness reigns a wonderful peace" [meaning, in spite of my ignorance of future events, my mind is at rest].[34] It is quite true that Teresa had shown she possessed that not uncommon gift of reading the minds of the people with whom she came into contact. Intuition, in that sense, is the result of unconscious observation. Whatever words we use to disguise our thoughts, we are betrayed in a thousand ways by minute signs. Not only do the face, the eyes, the voice, reveal the truth to the one who is looking for it, but the whole body speaks. The way we stand or walk, the nervous restlessness of hand and fingers, our manner of knocking at the door, of walking into the room, every muscle of ours whispers or shouts the truth and tells the observer what manner of man we are. He need not even consciously put together these signs and analyse them. He knows them by intuition. This undoubtedly explains some utterances of hers which, to the unreflecting, appear inexplicable. Her mind reading was unconscious observation. One of her visitors had said that, after her death, Pauline would be inconsolable. "Don't you believe it," said Teresa, "my sister will not have time to grieve over me. Until the end of her life she will be so busy on my account that she will not be able to suffer." To her

[33] N.V., p. 45.   [34] N.V., p. 184.

sister she said: "When I am dead, you will find your consolation in watching the letter box" (*du côté de la boîte aux lettres*).[35] This sounds like prophecy, indeed, and a prophecy which was amply fulfilled; but remember that Teresa knew her sister for the clear-headed, determined woman that she was and for a good organizer as well. They had had long conversations about the manuscript and doctrine of the Little Way. Teresa would not have been the intelligent young woman we take her for if she had not read accurately her sister's mind. Pauline was constantly asking leading questions which implied she was a saint. Pauline had persuaded her of the enormous importance of her book and of her new Way to perfection. She was taking notes daily of everything Teresa said or did, and there was so little secrecy about it that she would, on occasions, write down under her young sister's dictation. In these circumstances one need not assume the existence of divine inspiration and of a prophetic gift. Teresa, who, as a child, had made up her mind that she would be a great saint, could, without any difficulty, read her sister's thoughts on this point and her so-called "prophecy" could be more properly described as an intelligent anticipation of her sister's aims and exertions on her behalf.

Days and weeks went on, in pain, always in pain, in that unique reclusion of the sickroom, in that loneliness of spirit which is the forerunner and companion of death. Visitors came and went. Behind their apparently irrelevant chatter, Teresa sensed always the question that she would not answer: Are you a saint? At one time she says, "No, I am not a saint", then another time, "No, I do not believe that I am a *great saint*." And yet, after all, when she scrutinized her short life, she was quite certain now that she had never resisted God's will either in small or in great things. She knew that every Christian in a state of grace is technically a saint, that even the greatest sinner, if he repents, is in a limited sense a saint, even if he is only a temporary one.

Alone, much of the time with her three sisters, she slides

[35] Petitot, p. 117.

into their ways of thinking and of speaking. She talks to them naturally, without any restraint, in this new intimacy that she had not known since she had left *Les Buissonets*. She speaks her thoughts aloud. Why should she not? She was conscious of having received many and unusual spiritual gifts. She firmly hoped she would be saved. Might she not acknowledge it? One day, in August, about six weeks before she died, Marie, the eldest sister, reports this incident. She says: "I was close by her bed with Mother Agnès and Sister Geneviève. Suddenly, looking at us, she said very distinctly and with a heavenly expression on her face: 'You know very well that you are nursing a little saint.'" This was more definite than usual, but many times before and after that date she expressed herself again in terms that implied her belief in her own sainthood.

On June 9th, in answer to her sisters who said they would be so sad when she died, "Oh, no, you will see. I will let fall a shower of roses."[36] Alluding to the alleged apparition of a woman in white by the cradle of a newly baptized child, she said, "That is how I also shall go round then." When (on July 12th) someone asked: "You will look down on us from above, won't you?" The reply was: "No, I shall come down." On that same day she says to her sisters: "Do not believe that when I am in heaven you will have a happy time; it is not what I have had nor what I wished to have myself . . . but I shall send you lights." "If you knew all the plans I make, how many things I shall do when I am in heaven." Clearly, she even anticipated her canonization. "When roses were sent to her she would pluck their petals one by one, touching her crucifix lovingly with each. Once, when some of these petals fell on the ground, she said to us: gather them up carefully, they will serve one day to give pleasure to others. Do not lose a single one."[37]

[36] N.V., p. 35.

[37] Final perseverance is a gift of God more than a reward for our actions and the Council of Trent does not allow anyone to say with absolute and infallible certainty that he will have that great gift, unless he has learnt it by special revelation.

This is, we believe, a unique instance of a saint proclaiming their own sanctity and announcing their own canonization and we do not pretend we hold the key to this problem. Père Petitot acknowledges that her acute intelligence (he calls it genius) can, up to a point, explain her foresight. He quotes two examples of comparable prescience, one in Schopenhauer, who predicted that for a hundred years his teaching would not be appreciated, and the other in Stendhal, who announced that it was only towards the 1880's that his books would be read. Both predictions were correct and it shows that in these matters one must make a large allowance for the divining powers of men of genius. He adds: "Through a close study of Teresa's writings we have come to the conclusion that she was well endowed with one of the prerogatives of genius, that is an exact knowledge of herself and of her life's work." Is this explanation a full answer to our problem? Père Petitot acknowledges that it is not and as an additional solution suggests also an "interior revelation".

Teresa was not aware of having had any revelation. We have already seen her pressed on this point and answering: "I know no more than you know . . . I only guess through what I see and feel." Another day, to a suggestion of some special privilege, she replied: "Such [things] will never be my lot. Little souls could never imitate me in that." What kind of "interior revelation" can this be, which is not known as such to its recipient? It can only be a personal certainty; a very fragile foundation at any time, since the value of our certainties does not depend on their intensity, but on the good reasons we can show for them.

Let us add this observation. Even if we have been given the exact words uttered by Teresa in familiar conversation with her sisters, we do not always possess their full context, nor the mood in which Teresa was at the time, nor shall we ever know the tone of voice in which they were spoken. All these are points of importance if we wish to decide what Teresa had in her mind—"absolute certainty" or a wish and a hope.

THE LAST PHASE

Teresa, in the infirmary, was most of the time surrounded by her three sisters who took it for granted she was a saint, and their conversation implied it day after day. Teresa could not fail to be responsive to this atmosphere, and in all simplicity of mind, unfettered by any inhibitions, she expressed herself in the same words as they did. This was a firm hope in God rather than a gift of prophecy.

She was not uttering solemn declarations *urbi et orbi*, but only speaking her hopes and desires when she said in a language more poetical than theological, "I should be *unhappy in heaven* if I could not give some pleasure to those I love on earth." (But in *heaven God's will is our will and we cannot be unhappy*) or "I shall come down." "It will be like a rain of roses." (*Some people have looked for the fulfilment of this promise in a literal sense!*) The prose of Pauline is at times more imaginative than accurate. Has she by a slight touch of colour (*in inspired accents, with an angelic simplicity, with a celestial expression . . . etc.*)—an omission or an addition—put the wrong accent on the declarations of her sister?

At this distance it is impossible to say, but it seems to us that until the end, far from being sure she was already a saint, Teresa, in common with the rest of us, in common even with all the saints, did not yet feel secure and rested all her hopes on the succour of God. She did not really mean to announce to the world that she was a saint, but she hoped to be one and said so to her sisters.

We are in no lack of proofs regarding this uncertainty. During the last weeks of her life it is evident that Teresa was in a state of mind exactly the reverse of what one expects from someone who proclaims herself to be a saint. We have already laid much stress on the obsessional temptations of doubt that pursued her to the very last days, perhaps to her last moment on earth, but there is also much evidence of a feeling of insecurity—compatible, let us say it—with her will to believe, and a firm trust and hope in God. "Her soul," says Pauline, "was enveloped in thick darkness and her temptations against faith always conquered, but always returning robbed her of all feeling of happiness at the thought of approaching death."[38] On one occasion she said to her sister: "Last night I was seized with a terrible feeling of anguish; I was lost in darkness from out of which came an accursed voice: *Are you certain God loves you? Has He come to tell you so Himself? The opinion of a few creatures will not justify you in His sight.*" These two sentences have an obvious bearing on the question before us. She has been repeatedly told that she is a saint, but now the question, "Has He told you?" is left without an answer, because she had not had this answer revealed to her. "During August she was, so to speak, beside herself for several days and asked earnestly for prayers. We had never seen her in such a state. She kept repeating: 'Ah, if people only knew how the dying need their prayers.'" "One night she said to the infirmarian: 'The devil is beside me. I do not see him, but I feel him; he torments me and tries to drive me to despair . . . and I cannot pray. I can only look at our Blessed Lady. I can only say Jesus.'" "The startled infirmarian lighted a blessed candle and the spirit of darkness fled, never to return, but to the end the sufferer remained in a state of extreme anguish."[39] One must put side by side these texts and those we have quoted previously to obtain a balanced picture of the mind and intentions of Teresa.

These last few texts are taken from the *Epilogue* to the autobiography and they were written by Pauline, but the book *Novissima Verba* is just as explicit. Many sayings of Teresa express the same feelings of weakness, temptations, uncertainty. "Perhaps I am going to have delusions," (*Perdre mes idées*) she says on August 19th. "If you only knew [*how strange*] I feel." Pain affected her as it affects other patients. Once, after being in more violent pain than usual, she said to the infirmarian: "When the sick are in such torments, one should not leave within their reach any poisonous drugs; for in such agonies it does not take long for one to lose his reason." On another occasion, "You must pray for sick people

[38] E. p. 222. [39] E, p. 224.

when they are near death," she said to her sister. "If you only knew what goes on [*in their minds*]." In September "*inwardly* I am always on the rack". A few hours before her death: "I am exhausted. Oh! do pray for me. If you only knew. . . ." Through it all one perceives that anguish of mind that never left her: inwardly . . . on the rack! Where is the triumphant certainty that is usually attributed to her through those months of suffering?

She is not less great, not less admirable, because of those vacillations between the tortures of uncertainty and intimations of an immense glory to come. Her sanctity is not diminished because, like all human beings in face of death, like all the saints even, she feels darkness closing upon her, and only knows by faith that a more brilliant sun is about to rise and dissipate the shadows. To place a saint too much above human conditions, and beyond our imitation by artificial praise, does not help us, does not encourage us. We love more, because we come closer to, a saint who like ourselves is only a poor human being, a compound of darkness and light, yet showing us that, common clay as we are, we can rise to God and have some share in His Divinity.

V. QUALIS MATER, TALIS FILIA

The booklet of Pauline, *Novissima Verba*, would give us an overwhelming impression of self-absorption, almost of egotism, if we accepted it as a full account of the conversations that took place between the sisters. These "last sayings" are only a selection, and therefore we may be allowed to think that not infrequently their minds went back to the home where Teresa had spent eleven years, *Les Buissonnets*, and ever to those earlier days at Alençon when their mother was still alive. They cannot have forgotten these remarkable parents of theirs to whom they were so deeply indebted for their religious formation.

In fact the mother appears once, though briefly, in the

booklet. Pauline had something more than fading recollections of her and had kept many letters written to her and to Marie when they were in a convent boarding school and Teresa at home was still a baby. These letters were, naturally, full of those everyday happenings of which home life is made, and the baby's doings were given a prominent place in them. In one of these letters the mother pointed out that it was very difficult to find something new to say every week about Céline and Teresa. From this Pauline concluded that their mother must have invented or exaggerated the little pranks and bits of mischief of her small daughters in order to have a story to tell. To our mind, this is a glaring *non sequitur*, but Teresa agrees with this conclusion and remembers that before she was three she was very obedient and there was no need to scold her.

Informative as this may be about the babyhood of Teresa it does not tell us much about Madame Martin, but we should have to suppose these four sisters to be singularly devoid of natural feeling if, when they were together, they had kept a complete silence over one to whom they owed so much, one whom they resembled, each in important, though different characteristics.

Pauline and Teresa had both inherited their mother's religious sense, her uncommon will, her facile pen, but while the first exhibits also the same driving power and singleness of purpose, the same business and organizing abilities, we find in Teresa a mystical mind and a capacity to bear physical pain that reminds us of her mother. Writing to Marie and Pauline when Teresa was only ten months old, Madame Martin expresses the wish "to become a saint", just as her baby was going to do even before her first Communion. This was written at a time when she had on her hands the care of a large household and the entire management of a big lace business, and also when the cancer that carried her away was beginning to cause her some pain and anxiety.

In spite of intense sufferings, she tried to continue working to the end and almost succeeded. A few weeks before her death any kind of work became a physical impossibility, and it was only then that she resigned her lace-making business into the hands of her eldest daughter. Twenty years later Teresa was also to resolve—as her mother had done—to continue her usual occupations to the end. She said, "God does not give one desires that are incapable of fulfilment." She kept her resolve as long as she could stand on her feet, but her desire was not to be fulfilled. Her strength, not her courage, failed her, and the day came when she had to give in, and lie perforce inactive on a hospital bed.

Teresa has testified that she had always aimed at doing God's will in all things great or small. During her last illness, fearing that her prayers might express her own wishes, her own choice, she thought it best to ask neither for life nor for death, neither for more pain nor for less, but at all times to leave every decision to God's Providence. Madame Martin showed the same calm acceptance of the divine will as her daughter. It may have been, if anything, more admirable in the first than in the second, for Teresa had no personal responsibilities, while her mother had every right to be anxious about the future of her five young daughters—one of them a problem child—who needed guidance and love. Yet this is what she was writing to her sister-in-law six months before her death. "I am not frightened, I am very peaceful. I feel almost happy and I would not change my lot for any other whatsoever. . . . If God wills to cure me I shall be very glad for, in my heart, I want to live. It costs me much to leave my husband and my children. But, on the other hand, I feel myself that if I am not cured, it will be because, perhaps, it is more expedient for them that I go . . ."[40] "I am very peaceful," says the mother who knows that death is coming. "My soul is in a deep peace," says Teresa. They spoke the same words, because they had the same complete trust in God's Providence.

As long as the decision rested with her, Teresa had remained in her cell, in order to give less work to the Sisters, and more

[40] *The Story of a Family*, p. 203, by Rev. S. J. Piat, O.F.M.

rest at night to her neighbours. This was just what her mother twenty years earlier had done, confining herself to the most distant room in the house lest her family should be distressed by her groans and cries of pain during the sleepless hours of the night.

In the infirmary, Teresa had had to listen to the Sisters' speculations about her impending death. At home, her mother had had to listen to a brutal warning given by her own brother. On a visit to Alençon he told her point blank across the dinner table in front of the others: "My poor sister, you must not be under any illusions. Set your affairs in order, for you have no more than a month to live."

Teresa went through a very long illness, her mother through a longer one, and for both the last months were a time of excruciating suffering. Here again, at the end, they had something else in common: neither of them was given any relief from pain by those sedative drugs that are nowadays such a blessing to patients; the mother because morphia was not yet commonly used by doctors, the daughter because the Prioress would not permit it.

We could not have left the mother out of this last chapter of her daughter's story. The one—partly at least—explains the other. Who could say how much of her courage, of her serenity, or her religious spirit this valiant woman passed on to her daughter? Had she been different there might not have been a Saint Teresa, for the best gifts of God are poured out to us through the hands of men. Human beings, parents especially, are the ministers of His Providence. True, we are not the slaves of heredity any more than the slaves of circumstances. We can rise above them. We can make our destiny —up to a point. We are free to choose—up to a point; but behind us all stand the multitudes of our ancestors who through the unpredictable and mysterious alchemy of heredity, have each of them passed on to us something of their characteristics of mind and body, of their inclinations, good and bad. If in the course of the long centuries one of their race rises above the rest of humanity, a flower in a barren desert, then the obscure and unimportant existence of all the others has had its justification. Because Zélie Martin was the mother of Teresa, a reflection of her daughter's glory will for ever shine over her, and, because of her, she will not be forgotten.

VI. MY GOD, I LOVE THEE

One year earlier, on the eve of Good Friday, when the first warning of her condition had come to Teresa, "thinking that she was going to die that night, her heart almost broke with joy". Had she known of the long, cruel journey in front of her, her heart might have been broken not with joy, but with fear. What did she know of death? She had seen old Mother Geneviève go, but hers had been the easy death of the very old, to whom it comes as gently as sleep, and had been made almost picturesque by the ceremonial that surrounded it. During the epidemic of influenza in 1891-2 quite a few members of the community had disappeared, but in such a quiet, almost discreet, way that it was no more impressive than the somewhat hurried departure of a traveller for some distant country. Teresa tells us how one morning she had found Sister Magdalen lying fully dressed on her bed, dead. She was neither shocked nor surprised, but calmly went to fetch a blessed candle and then placed a wreath of roses on her head.

Can we wonder at her romantic way of hailing death at that time as "the joyful approach of the Bridegroom", as the day when "she would join her Beloved in His beautiful heaven"? She did not know that from then onwards the very thought of heaven would become a doubt and a torment; that until the end, not in the blinding light of certainty and raptures, but by faith and will alone, would she remain close to this Beloved; that even the consolation of Holy Communion would be refused to her at the time of her death and for many weeks before. She had not even any inkling of the terrible form tuberculosis could take and would take for her before the end. When the time came she showed herself to be the true daughter of Zélie Martin.

Another unforeseen trial preceded the final act of the tragedy. We have already alluded[41] to the struggle for power between Pauline and Mother Marie de Gonzague. In February 1893 the latter was deprived of her post by the election of her rival, and for three years had the humiliation of serving under her orders. The next election, in March 1896, was prepared by Mother Marie de Gonzague by intense canvassing, and resulted in her re-election as Prioress. But the contest, conducted with the acidulated sweetness of convent politics, nearly resulted in failure and it was only after seven successive ballots that the choice of the vacillating Sisters decided against Pauline. This half success rankled. It was a bad omen, and Mother de Gonzague resolved to make her position safe for the future. She planned sending away both Pauline and Céline to Indo-China, only leaving the inoffensive Teresa and Marie tó deal with. She did not keep her intentions secret, and Teresa had to face the possibility of losing her two favourite sisters at the moment when she might need them more than ever. Their threatened departure distressed her all the more because she knew that the reasons for their intended removal were pitifully selfish and petty. If we enter into these inglorious details, it is because they give us a chance to admire the greatness of Teresa's spirit. It was not enough for her to speak of the Prioress with much exaggerated praise, as if she had been a very angel, but at the infirmary she said she would be glad to die in her arms because, with Pauline, it would have given her a natural satisfaction that she wished to deny herself.

The anxieties of Teresa about the possible departure of her two favourite sisters were all the harder to bear on account of the enfeebled state of her health, for the disease continued its unchecked progress as summer and winter went by. It

[41] Chap. VII, Section II.

was during the autumn of 1896 that, one morning, Pauline, running up to her cell after Mass, found her sister speechless and exhausted. We have already related the final incident which, in the early spring, forced the hands of the Prioress, that night after Matins, when it took Teresa an hour to drag herself from chapel to cell, and then another hour to take off her dress. Her fingers, numb and trembling with fever and cold, would not do their service and unfasten strings and buttons.

As a rule, in a small community of women, there is very little that escapes general attention and interested comment. Incredible as it sounds, we are asked to believe that up to this time nobody knew Teresa was ill. Years afterwards, when they had to give evidence, they all declare solemnly that to the best of their knowledge, before April 1897, Teresa was not ill.[42] Does it mean that these women who lived under the same roof took no interest whatever in one another? Or were they totally unobservant and completely indifferent to one another's troubles? It may be that, on this point at least, their memory had grown uncertain after so many years and they had to refresh it in the confabulations that must have taken place among them previous to the collection of evidence for Rome. This would, no doubt, explain their unanimity. Or, is it that during the Process, realizing they had been dealing with a saint, they were one and all trying in advance to repudiate all accusations of neglect?

Père A. Noché, S.J., in his book, *La réponse des textes et des archives*, unreservedly accepts the view that no one knew Teresa was ill, and even goes so far as to affirm that Teresa did not consider herself a sick woman. Yet, on the same page, seven lines above, he writes that Teresa, early in 1897, said she expected to die that year.[43]

I must here let the reader make up his mind as to what and whom he is to believe.

In fairness to the Prioress and Sisters let it be said that, as far as we can see, this was exactly what Teresa had intended,

[42] C, p. 397 and note 38.   [43] C, p. 401.

what she had deliberately chosen. She meant them all to be deceived as to the real state of her health, because otherwise they might have interfered with her intention to keep going to the last possible minute. At last, after the incident related above, she had to confess herself beaten and take into her confidence Sister Marie de la Trinité, who, in turn, warned the Prioress and Pauline. At last the Prioress and Sisters managed to perceive a fact that had been evident for a long time: Teresa *was ill*. From then onwards she was treated as an invalid and nursed according to the inefficient methods of the day. For two months longer, by her own wish, she remained in her cell and was nursed there. On sunny days she would be taken down to the garden and, in an invalid chair, sit in a warm corner among the flowers she loved. Occasionally she would take a short walk, just a few steps, but she found this exhausting.

Once she joined the Sisters in front of a garden shrine and sang a hymn with them—or tried to. It was there, in the open air, that, in June, she wrote the last chapters of her biography; those addressed to the Prioress. It was in June also that Céline took the last photographs of her sister and that the gardener heard her gasping, "Oh, do hurry up. I am exhausted."

Soon, they realized she could not recover, and in July they even expected her to die any day. They were mistaken. These daily feverish attacks that left her spent and shivering, this cough that shook her through the long hours of the night and robbed her of sleep and rest, the frequent hæmorrhages which frightened them, were only a prelude. She had long ago prayed that suffering might be her portion and her wish was to be amply granted. For three more months she was to be severely tried, in her mind by doubt and in her body by some unexpected complications of her illness.

On July 8th they carried her downstairs on a mattress and, as they laid her on a bed in the infirmary, she noticed they had moved there the statue of the Virgin which had smiled at her and healed her nervous complaint when she was a child. Perhaps they had some hope of a miraculous cure. Teresa looked at her beloved statue just in front of the bed, but her soul was, as usual, plunged in darkness. Gazing at it she wept and said, "Never has she seemed more beautiful." "Then, why are you crying?" said her sister Marie. "Is it because of the consolation it gives you?" "Yes, but now [*what I see*] it is only a statue, whereas you know well that then it was not." "Are you still in the night of faith?" [That is, tormented by doubts.] "Ah! Am I not!"[44]

This was Teresa's first day in the infirmary, and this little episode confirms what we know otherwise, that, from that moment to her last day on earth, this disease of doubt was to give her no respite. It would, to the end, confuse her mind and sadden her heart, though it would not weaken her will to believe. At first these doubts were concerned only about the existence of heaven and the survival of the soul, but the logic of facts would extend them to the whole edifice of her faith. If there be no reward for the just, then, where is the justice of God? And if there be no justice, then, how can there be a God? She never gave in to these thoughts. One morning, after a difficult night when she had been tormented by them, she said, "I have been making acts of faith the whole time." It requires little imagination to form some idea of the mental torture this conflict caused Teresa when she knew that death could not be far away.

On July 30th they thought she would not live through the night. The priest was sent for and the whole community assembled to join in the prayers that accompany the rite of anointing. On this occasion it is usual for the sick Sister to ask solemnly for the forgiveness of her former companions for any offence she may have given them.

As they expected her to die that same night, the infirmarians were soon busy making the usual preparations. They brought

---

[44] We have here blended two accounts together, the one in the *Epilogue* and the other in a document preserved in the archives of the convent. At first they do not seem to tally but on examination the question about "the night of faith" and the remark, "it is only a statue" agree and make the sense clear.

down the rough mattress on which the body was to be laid and left it outside the door and Teresa saw it. Having heard of the box of lilies that had been sent for the decoration of the mortuary chapel, she insisted they should be shown to her. It seemed to give her a childish pleasure to look at them, to handle them, and she kept on repeating: "This is all for me, all for me." Some bustle in the adjoining room warned her that they were bringing in the holy water stoup and brush and the blessed candles from the sacristy, and she insisted they should be shown her. She looked at them complacently and, as the nuns round her bed, perhaps under a great strain, seemed inclined to cry, she made up an amusing description of her funeral in order to make them smile. When it came to the candle, she added, "You will give it me to hold, but please, I won't have the candlestick, it's too ugly."

This levity will perhaps shock some of us who would expect Teresa to play the part of a saint on the point of death with more gravity and to distribute words of edification all round. To such we recommend the last pages of the *Epilogue*. Their solemnity, their flamboyant poetry will, we feel certain, satisfy them. Pauline must have taken much trouble over these pages for her later versions are more florid than the earlier ones.

Somehow we are under the impression that Pauline had little sense of humour, and that she mistook an amusing piece of fooling on the part of Teresa for a pronouncement of ponderous gravity. As an example of this we might take, in *Novissima Verba* (under July 20th), the description of the dinner of the Holy Family served by Teresa: sweets for the bambino, to the Virgin some ripe peaches and to St. Joseph a glass of rum with the comment, "Poor St. Joseph, it will do him a lot of good." What was intended to be funny is turned into an edifying anecdote.

Many of us will recall the last joke of St. Thomas More as he was laying his head on the block. Some of the people present were shocked. They thought he was showing an unseemly levity at that solemn moment. Thomas More knew

THE LAST PHASE

better. Why should we expect saints to go about with a long face?

Soon, however, a time came when Teresa would have found it hard to see the humorous side of a funeral. Some unforeseen complications set in, and the disease, before finishing its work on the lungs, found its way to the digestive tract. Each time Teresa had to be propped up in order to ease a fit of coughing, she felt as if she were sitting on a chair of red-hot iron. When she drank a glass of water she said it was like pouring fire into a glowing furnace. Extensive bed-sores developed; and there was no relief, no comfort, to be found day or night in any position. Her soul continued in "darkness and bitter anguish" and more so when she was seeking refuge in prayer. "When I cry to heaven for help, it is then I feel most abandoned." Soon she could only say: "Oh, my God, oh, my God, I can do no more, have mercy on me, have mercy on me." Her condition roused pity in anyone who came near. They would make clumsy attempts, with consoling words, to raise her spirits. What does one know about the feelings of even one's closest friends? Words are poor tokens and fail equally to describe their pain or our sympathy. Teresa, on her death-bed, knew the shallowness of all the eloquent maxims about pain elaborated by authors who have never experienced it. "Oh, Mother!" she said, "what is the good of writing beautiful things about suffering. It means nothing, nothing! When you are going through it, then you know the worthlessness of all this eloquence."

It was at the time when her own sufferings became intolerable, at the time when more than ever she needed the comforting presence of her Divine Lover that she was denied it. Her frequent blood vomitings made Communion impossible and she received it for the last time on August 19th.

It seemed that henceforth every kind of spiritual consolation was denied her. Her faith remained unshakable and she bore the tragic sufferings of the last weeks as she had borne the lesser ones of convent life for the love of God. Her absolute trust in Him gave her a profound peace that went deeper than doubts and deeper than physical sufferings. She would not pray either for more pain or for less, either for recovery or for death. "What God chooses for me is also what pleases me best," she said, and in the midst of pain she believed in His love: "I do not regret to have loved Him."

Yet, she felt now as one forsaken. The heavens seemed closed to her, darkness surrounded her as if she were in a tomb. "Look over there," she said to Pauline, "that corner of the garden, under the chestnut trees, how black it is, like a well of darkness. In such deep shadows I lie body and soul, and not a shaft of light can penetrate my gloom. But I lie there in peace." "I pray to the saints, I appeal for help. They seem deaf and blind; they do not answer me." In those lonely hours, when dying people grope unseeingly for their friends' hands, she put out her extended arms for her sisters to hold on each side of the bed and remained there for a while like a crucified victim.

At last the end was drawing near. This was the 29th of September. Over her came that feeling of utter weakness, of infinite lassitude, that weariness of mind which turns the strongest patient into an obedient child. She turned to the Prioress and anxiously asked her, "Is this the agony?" "What must I do? How does one die?" "I am sure I shall not know how to die . . . is it for to-day, Mother? . . . Ah! if only I could die now, just now, how glad I should be." "Pray for me." "I can do no more. . . . Oh! if you knew." But no one knows, for we have so few words, such feeble words to express our deepest emotions, to explain our most violent sensations, like anguish or love, or pain or happiness! The day went on slowly. All had been said; she had nothing more to say.

Her immense vitality kept her going for another night. Pauline, by her bedside, was watching. The night had been one of unceasing pain, and Teresa's soul was still in that land of darkness where the eye discerns no light, no heaven, no anything. The presence of her sister reminded her of the

THE LAST PHASE

repeated suggestion that she would die in a glorious apotheosis of love. Looking at the statue of the Virgin in front of her, opposite the bed, she exclaimed, "I have prayed to her, oh! so fervently, but what I feel is just the pangs of the agony unmixed with any kind of consolation." She remained silent most of the time. Once, however, later in the day, she roused herself and tried to sit up, saying, "See how strong I am still. No, I am not going to die, this may go on for months yet, months of suffering; I gladly accept them."

During the few hours that remained, her spirit was no more spared than her body. Her Divine Friend hid Himself, kept an unbroken silence and did not send her any of those little signs for which she used to ask as tokens of His continued love. All through these hours of darkness she held her crucifix and kept looking at it constantly, her mind fixed on her Saviour in trusting confidence, and every word she said testified that she did not weaken in her resolve to accomplish His will and to suffer as long as He would permit.

Later in the afternoon, the nuns, called by the convent bell, assembled in the sick room to assist her by their prayers, but, after two hours had passed without any change, the Prioress sent them away. "Am I not to die yet?" asked Teresa and, when she was told it might not be for a while, she answered, "Very well, very well, be it so. I do not wish to suffer less."

It was seven o'clock when a sudden change came over her, announcing that the end was near, and the bell summoned the Sisters for the second time. Unaware of her surroundings, Teresa kept her eyes fixed on her crucifix. Even at this supreme moment, when the visible world around her was already sinking into the shadows of night, this other darkness which had for so long enveloped her soul and confused her spirit, had not lifted. She had never wavered, never surrendered to her haunting doubts, and she did not falter at the end. Now, in the face of death, gathering all her strength, all her faith, all her love, she voiced with her last breath her vehement protest that the silence of God had not touched her faith nor diminished her love, and they heard her speak, "Oh! I love Him. My God, I love You."

These were her last words. Her head fell back on the pillows: she never spoke again. This was the 30th day of September, 1897.

She was then twenty-four years and nine months old and she had spent in Carmel nine years and six months of her life.

APPENDICES

APPENDIX I

GILDING REFINED GOLD

OUR narrative should have ended here. Seen at close quarters neither sickness nor death is poetical or pretty, and we cannot see the point in bringing out physical details that belong to the sick room and have no bearing on the story. The choice, unfortunately, has not been left to us.

If one is happy enough to die among those who love him, their affection will retain but a blurred image of those last reflex actions of muscles and nerves which are common enough when life is just flickering out. One does not discuss these distressing features of death with strangers. Pauline, however, took another line altogether, and around a few involuntary muscular contractions weaved a pretty story of heavenly visions. Since Teresa could not speak she even puts into her mouth some edifying speeches.[1]

A story does not become true because it sounds pretty, and, before accepting it or rejecting it, the historian's duty is to examine closely an account which even at first sight looks like the beginning of a legend.

Let us first write down a bare statement of the facts that we accept, without the embellishments that were later on added to them.

Immediately after Teresa had spoken her last words her frame relaxed, her head, resting on the pillow, inclined a little to the right. The Sisters present thought it was all over.[2]

[1] In the early editions only.
[2] We put together the accounts found in *Novissima Verba* and in the Epilogue of *The Story of a Soul*.

A few moments later she re-opened her eyes, this time not looking at her crucifix or at anyone, but staring upwards with the unseeing intensity that warns us that the mind is no longer in control of the senses. This lasted about one minute or less.[3] Meanwhile, the last straining efforts of the breathing mechanism jerked the head feebly a few times. Marie Guérin, her cousin, who was present, wondering whether this was already the final terrible stare of death, moved a candle to and fro before the eyes without inducing a flicker. Then, according to Pauline, the eyes closed again, and this time for ever.

Shall we see in these purely reflex movements the proof that Teresa had a vision during that last minute of her life and that she died "in transports of love" as Pauline would have us believe?

The improbable is not the same thing as the impossible, and we cannot rule out without examination what Pauline affirms with so much poetical force. Let us remember, however, that private visions and the like can never be an object of Catholic faith and must be adjudicated upon according to evidence, common experience, and rules of human prudence.

We are therefore going to try and assess first the credibility of the witness and afterwards the intrinsic value of the evidence. We consider that we are fully entitled to do so.

Let us study our witness. We are not going to object to Pauline on the general grounds that women are too imaginative to make reliable witnesses, nor that one who has made up his mind as to what he is going to see, is likely to see it. Pauline might be the exception. But we do say that a mere opinion about the expression of somebody's eyes or face, unsupported by other circumstantial evidence, would hardly be accepted as proof in an English court. Such a testimony is necessarily highly coloured by what one expects or even desires to read on that face and in those eyes. If the witness can also be shown to be a highly imaginative person, what importance can be attached to her testimony.

[3] The space of a *Credo*. One can say the Creed in less than one minute without haste.

Pauline was like her mother, a practical woman. She was also, again like her mother, an imaginative one. We can take as a general sign of this disposition, not only the fanciful style of the last pages of the *Epilogue*, but the repeated attempts at introducing one bird after another in the accounts of her sister's death. She is trying to put a pretty sentimental frame round the grim picture of death. It was easy enough since, given a garden and a few trees, one is likely to hear the twittering of birds. In an early edition of *The Story of a Soul*, the birds chosen were a linnet and a canary. It is not suggested they were the descendants of that linnet and that canary which young Teresa had kept in captivity at home, but there seems to be a happy coincidence of names. In more recent editions the two birds have disappeared, possibly because, in French, their names are not used in a complimentary sense. (*Quel serin! Tête de linot.*) They make room in *Novissima Verba* for a gathering of birds (unspecified) who, during the whole afternoon of September 30th, sang lustily in a tree near the infirmary window. In the Epilogue of *The Story of a Soul* all these birds are discarded in favour of a dove, a cooing dove, which, of course, has, over the others, the advantage of possessing scriptural associations. We find this insistent pursuit of postcard prettiness difficult to associate with the cold observation and the impartial presentation of facts that are expected from one who is writing history. Romance will probably intrude somewhere, and in effect it does when, on the next page,[4] we are treated to stories of ghostly kisses, celestial perfumes (denied by Céline) and floating crowns. The paragraph relating these marvels was not included in the earlier editions. It is an afterthought.

Have we not already noted in the chapter, "I am a saint", that for months past Pauline had been haunted by the idea that her sister must have "a beautiful death"? As early as the fourth of June, it is evident that Teresa has been sounded on this point, catechized almost. On that day Teresa answers Céline, who has spoken of angels round her death-bed, and

[4] E, p. 241.

says, "She would like to have a beautiful death if that could give her sisters any pleasure!" But one can feel she is also answering some previous unreported conversation. "Do not feel pained if at the moment of death I do not show any signs of happiness." There are a few such answers to unrecorded promptings (July 5th, July 15th) and, at last, Pauline comes out in the open with the text of St. John of the Cross—to which repeated allusions had been made—about dying in admirable transports of love.[5]

We cannot therefore be in any way surprised when we find that Pauline makes her story fit in with the poetical description of a saint's death by the Spanish mystic. Whether it fits in with the facts is a different question.

The story was told by Pauline more than once and each account differs from the others in small, but not unimportant, particulars. To begin with—the action of Marie Guérin moving a candle to and fro before the eyes of Teresa was left out both in *The Story of a Soul* and in *Novissima Verba*. It only appears in the *Summarium* (p. 830). Why this silence?

In the English translation of *The Story of a Soul*, Mgr. Thomas N. Taylor says that "after Teresa had spoken her last words she raised herself". [*Elle se releva.*] According to the deposition of Pauline found in the *Summarium*, she opened her eyes [*elle leva les yeux*] and the *Novissima Verba* merely says "her eyes were directed upwards [*fixes en haut*]". *The Story of a Soul* says "she fixed her gaze a little above the statue of Our Lady [which was just in front of the bed]". Do you see the process? The eyes, on opening, were directed towards the ceiling but the statue somehow had to be brought in. It adds to the dramatic effect.

Her eyes, says *The Story of a Soul*, "shone with unutterable joy", while the text of *Novissima Verba* tells us of "irradiated eyes speaking of a bliss beyond all her expectations". Meanwhile, mind you, practical Marie Guérin, unimpressed by the "irradiated" eyes, the bliss and the unutterable joy, and only wondering whether Teresa was conscious or not, was mov-

[5] *Les assauts délicieux que leur livre l'amour.*

ing a candle to and fro across her face. If the account of Pauline was correct, then Marie Guérin's action looks singularly irreverent, and during that one minute or less prevented the others from making very accurate observations.

The convulsive tremors of the head, probably caused by the last gasping efforts for breath, are given by Pauline a poetical explanation (*Novissima Verba*) which we cannot afford to miss. Listen: "Her head was executing certain movements and it looked as if someone had repeatedly wounded her with the shafts of love."

In the early editions we were treated to a speech which Teresa could not make, and which Pauline makes for her: she seemed to say: "Here is my God coming near. The sight of His divine beauty is more than I can bear . . . my dream has come true . . . I die of love!" This has been discarded in later editions, but there remains quite enough for us to see what can be done by a romantic soul who interprets the reflex movements of an unconscious person with the sure knowledge that the dead cannot criticize their historians.

We have given our account. We must not deny the reader the pleasure of having that of Pauline. We take it from the English version of the autobiography, p. 240, with the exception of the text of St. John of the Cross which we translate literally from the French.

"Scarcely had she spoken when, to our great surprise, her whole frame drooped quite suddenly, her head inclined a little to the right in the attitude of the virgin martyrs offering themselves to the sword; or rather as a victim of Love, awaiting from the Divine Archer the fiery shaft by which she longs to die. All at once, she raised herself, as though called by a mysterious voice, and, opening her eyes, which shone with unutterable joy, she fixed her gaze a little above the statue of Our Lady, and so remained for the space of a *Credo*, when her blessed soul, the prey of the 'Divine Eagle' was borne away to the heights of heaven.

"May we not apply to her that sublime prophecy of St. John of the Cross, referring to souls consumed by the fire of Divine Love? 'They die in the midst of admirable transports and of the raptured onslaughts of love.'"⁶ Truly, a writer of imagination is a creator, for he can make something out of nothing! Let us add that Céline, the painter, who has rectified the photos of her sister, has also translated the above story into pictorial form.

⁶ (*Elles meurent dans des transports admirables et des assauts delicieux que leur livre l'amour.*)

APPENDIX II

STYLE AND PERSONALITY
ST. TERESA'S PROSE AND VERSE

BOOKS, almost necessarily, reveal something of the personality of their authors. We do not mean their intellectual gifts alone, but the turn of their minds and their very character. To some readers, this is their principal attraction. A man to whom writing is a natural medium of expression will have some kind of style that we recognize as his own. Like many bells which may be giving forth the same note of the scale while the tone of each is different, so also a man's style is the tone that betrays his personality. Style is no accident; it is less a choice of words than a manner of thinking, a manner of feeling: that is, the man himself. If we study the style of St. Teresa we shall soon be in contact with her real self. What she chooses to say and her manner of saying it reveals her at least as clearly as the recorded impressions of those who knew her.

The Story of a Soul is, in some important respects, a very remarkable book. It is a piece of self-revelation which has the unusual quality of absolute sincerity. Teresa tells us about herself as far as she knew, remembered and understood her motives. Her feelings are as fully analysed as she was able and, since she was a very intelligent and very clear-headed woman, the book she wrote is a first-class human document It would not, however, be doing her a service to compare it with the Confessions of St. Augustine. This Doctor of the Church, besides being a great thinker, had been a teacher of eloquence and had had a long training in the proper use of words. Teresa had had no such training and besides, when she wrote the last chapters, in pain of body and weariness of soul, she had only four months to live. She was racing death, and did not know whether time would be given her to finish the course. In fact, she was never able to revise her work. Handicapped as she was, she gives us, nevertheless, a glimpse of what she might have done in more favourable circumstances. When she relates an anecdote she does it with the conciseness, the restraint, and the sure selection of telling incident that belong to the born writer. As Flaubert gives us a vivid impression of the stillness of death by telling us of a fly moving across the eyelashes of a dead woman, so Teresa, in order to make us see how the meaning of death was made plain to her when she lost her mother, drew this brief but unforgettable picture. She tells us of a baby of four, herself, creeping up the stairs and coming face to face with the coffin standing upright in the passage: "I was so small that I had to lift up my head to see its whole length, and it seemed a huge and melancholy thing."

And likewise the story of old Mother St. Peter or even that of a little argument—perhaps more heated than it should have been—that took place outside the infirmary between herself and another Sister, are supremely well told. She had undoubtedly a gift that would have been worth cultivating.

Shall we go further and join the ranks of those enthusiasts who speak of her genius and give her prose and verse an unjustified and extravagant praise? Her writings, says one, "sometimes rival the finest French prose", and another, Père Fl. Jubaru, S.J., in the preface of her book of *Poésies*, declares that "in her admirable *Story of a Soul* one finds pages equal to the most brilliant, the warmest, the highest and the richest in our beautiful and crystal clear French language". We regret to say that we cannot share Père Fl. Jubaru's lyrical transports. Writing is a craft which has to be learned. St. Teresa had gifts, but was not given the time or opportunity to develop them. In other circumstances, she might have become a professional writer. When she is telling a story or giving practical advice her style is generally terse, clear and to the point; her comparisons are sometimes striking. Speaking of some abnormal forms of physical mortification, she says, "Use them but sparingly. Pride and self-will have generally more to do with it than virtue."[1] Some nuns were in the habit of exchanging pious letters with earnest young priests, and thought they were doing wonders. Judging by samples which have come our way, this correspondence was one of emotional platitudes and bad theology on both sides. Teresa deprecated this practice strongly. " In Carmel we must not coin bad money in order to buy souls. Often it is that fine words written and fine words received are but an exchange of counterfeit coins."[2] This is very neatly said.

When she finds herself in the grip of a genuine and intense emotion, her style becomes personal and rises to corresponding heights. She can move the reader because she herself is moved. For the last eighteen months of her life, she endured the most grievous and unexpected trial that a saint could suffer: that of doubt. She was already rejoicing at the prospect of death, at the thought of meeting her Beloved, when suddenly the lamps went out, she found herself in a land of darkness. Was heaven a dream, and this life alone a reality? Read those pages where she tells us of her plight and then say, if you can, that your heart has not been stirred to the depths.

On the other hand her style is very often emotional, not to say dramatic, when there is no adequate reason for it. At the convent, Teresa seems to have kept a never relaxed control on her words and actions; but in her writings her sensitive and highly strung temperament is much in evidence.

Here is a telling but not isolated instance of it. Having secured her father's consent to enter the convent—she was then only fourteen—she confides her secret to her uncle Guérin. Very sensibly, he points out that to become a cloistered nun at fifteen is contrary to human prudence and that he will oppose her unreasonable plans. At this point the biography devotes a whole page to the description of her

[1] N.V., p. 110.   [2] N.V., p. 57.

feelings: "Her heart is overwhelmed with grief . . . she endures a three days' martyrdom of the most grievous kind. She was lost in a fearful desert. All around was night, dark night, utter desolation, death."[3] As she protests she is only seeking the will of God, these explosions of despair seem rather astonishing. They are renewed at each obstacle, when the bishop refuses to take her seriously, and even when the Pope assures her that, "If it be God's will, it will be done." Then, "her sorrow is crushing . . . all is over . . . her heart is pierced. . . ." She seems to speak of her sorrows with the bitter relish of the neuropath who enjoys feeling his feelings.

This exaggeration of language can be observed on many trifling occasions; on this one, for instance, when Céline and herself, like a pair of tomboys, scrambled over stones and rubbish at the Coliseum, in order to reach the arena, while their old father was calling loudly, but in vain, for them to return. Thereupon Teresa speaks " of the *fatigue and dangers* they had to face to reach the goal of their desires and of their *perilous ascent* on their return journey". After all, this was not the conquest of Mount Everest! She tells us that her time of spiritual direction, with the Mistress of Novices—whom she liked—was "a torture and a real martyrdom"; hyperbole or nerves?

On the morning when, as a postulant, she entered Carmel, and as she led the way to the door of her future home, "The beating of my heart," she says, "became so violent that I wondered if I were going to die. Oh! the agony of that moment." That moment! Surely she cannot have believed she was going to die when her dearest wishes were being fulfilled. She was dramatizing.

We could give many instances of similar exaggerations unwarranted by the circumstances from which they sprang.

On the other hand here is another puzzle, and one of which we do not possess the key. All her thoughts revolved, all her emotions centred, on that love for Jesus Christ which filled her mind and heart almost to the exclusion of everything else.

[3] E, p. 96.

STYLE AND PERSONALITY

We should expect her writing to be at its very best in descriptions of religious experiences, and a writer of genius would, if need be, have created his own language under the stress of emotion. What happens? Here and there we find a happy sentence, but generally speaking, at the very time when we expect her to be original, we find her using a vocabulary that is artificial, conventional and imitative. All the devotional aspirations of Teresa are expressed in a ready-made vocabulary: blood, lambs, holocausts, ineffable love, celestial looks, hearts, transports, flames and furnaces. The language is forcible enough but artificial. She speaks repeatedly of dying of love, of martyrs of love. She writes: "I had longed to give sinners to drink of the Blood of the Immaculate Lamb that it might wash away their stains. . . ." Or: "I poured out the precious blood of Jesus upon souls, and that I might quench His thirst, I offered to Jesus these same souls refreshed with the dew of Calvary." To the average reader, all this sounds unreal, not to say irritating. This phraseology has been used so often and so glibly and by people who meant so little by it, that, like an old coin, it is worn and defaced and one can only make a guess at its actual value.

When one begins to use this impassioned language, one does not come down to earth easily, one has to keep up the same level. Poetical flights must be expected and by this we mean lilies and roses, birds and dawn and blue skies, all the stock in trade of very young persons. In the first page of *The Story of a Soul* we are told of the brilliance of the rose and the whiteness of the lily which do not lessen the perfume of the violet. She herself is "like a flower after the storm". And then "the little flower speaks", "our Lord allowed her to see the light in a holy soil fragrant with the odour of purity He caused eight fair lilies [*her brothers and sisters*] to spring there before she appeared."

This poetry is generally sentimental in an imitative way which makes one wonder how much represents real sentiment and how much is purely reminiscent of the consumptive, mournful and self-pitying poetry of the first half of the nineteenth century. When Teresa goes out fishing with her father, she soon draws aside some distance away. (She may be at that time six or seven years old.) "My reflections are really deep[4] . . . my soul is absorbed in prayer. Far-off sounds wafted towards me on the murmuring breeze and faint notes of music from the neighbouring town, *tinged my thoughts with sweet melancholy.*" Père Petitot calls this, "sentimental and Lamartinian". We agree. This artificial writing had been out of fashion for fifty years but was still admired at Lisieux.

The narrative of the journey to Rome is sprinkled with aesthetic judgments and moral reflections. The first are such as one can expect to find from the pen of a girl of fourteen; the second are not. She speaks of the "exalted titles of her travelling companions" as "a vapour of smoke" and realizes that "true greatness is not found in a name but in the soul". After admiring the mountain scenery of Switzerland, she reflects that after all: "This is a land of exile destined to endure but a day." These conventional considerations were still in fashion, as much in France as in Victorian England, when Teresa was a child and writers were fond of interlarding their stories with moralizings. When Teresa is just herself, and writes as she feels, she can do much better than this.

Does *The Story of a Soul* belong to literature? Yes, if publishing figures are taken as a guide and a criterion. And so would *Mein Kampf* by the same test. But it seems to us that the imposing sales of St. Teresa's *Story of a Soul* are only an index of popularity, not one of literary merit. Sales and fame do not always run along the same paths as literature or philosophy. Let us concede that the flowery language, the riot of emotion, the intense manner of the autobiography, is to many people a pure delight. It gives them the same

[4] Compare the "deep thoughts and sweet melancholy" of Teresa with the plain statement of Joan of Arc as a child when she left her companions and their games in order to pray: "I am going to talk with God."

artistic enjoyment as, say, the absurd and popular picture of Teresa dying in the raptured ecstasies of love. On the other hand we must put on record that, at least in England, our taste runs on more sober and realistic lines. The saint herself had found most books of devotion unreadable. Likewise, some good judges have confessed to us that the style of *The Story of a Soul* made them close it after a few pages. We shall leave it at that, while bearing in mind that emotional style, used occasionally, can be extremely impressive, but used constantly it puts the reader on his guard. It becomes a clue to the writer's temperament, and is also a warning that over-emphatic statements must be examined with care before they are taken literally.

We cannot leave the "poems" of St. Teresa out of the picture for they have been commended in the same superlative and unreserved terms as her prose. In his preface to them, Père Jubaru, S.J., tells us that: "One cannot read these poems without being impressed with the intellectual culture, the delicacy of taste, the nobility of feeling they reveal. They give one a high notion of the intellectual and literary level one finds in our Carmelite convents, etc. . . ."[5] Exaggerations of this sort oblige one to protest in the name of common sense. No one will contest the sincerity and the depth of feeling of St. Teresa's writings, but earnestness and emotion are no substitute for poetical power.

St. Teresa seems to have attached a great importance to her verse. All poets do. Our candid opinion is that a good half of her compositions could have remained unpublished without loss to anyone and that the other half is no poetry but rhymed prose, not a proof of talent but a token of earnestness. These "poems", we must remember, were meant to be sung, not read, and they are no better and no worse than the average hymns. In reading them one is aware that the severe discipline of metre and rhyme was, most of the time, too much for the poet. It happened also that, tormented by scruples and doubts, she wrote at times without joy or inspiration "of

[5] Preface to the Poems of St. Teresa, pp. VI and VII.

what she wished to believe ". (These are her own words.) Such moments are not propitious to poets.

Very occasionally a good line, a good stanza, occurs in which there is no padding, no superfluous adjectives, but instead, a compressed yet clear and well-expressed thought. But, for one lucky verse, how many should never have been printed? Unless we gave examples that illustrate our meaning, we might be accused of prejudice or injustice. Out of a long list of possibles, let us quote some lines of *L'Abandon* and of the *Hymn to the Holy Face*.

> " *Il est sur cette terre*
> *Un arbre merveilleux*
> *Sa racine, ô mystère*
> *Se trouve dans les cieux;*
> *Là sans craindre l'orage*
> *On peut se reposer.*
>
> *De cet arbre ineffable*
> *L'Amour, voilà le nom.*"[6]

Ineffable and marvellous indeed must be this inverted tree, which is love and under which you can sit and rest.

Now let us quote a few lines of the *Hymn to the Holy Face*:

> " *Ta face est ma seule patrie*
> *Elle est mon royaume d'amour*
> *Elle est ma riante prairie*
> *Mon doux soleil de chaque jour*
> *Elle est le lys de la vallée . . .*" etc.[7]

Thus, the Holy Face can be a mother country, a kingdom of love, a smiling meadow, sweet sunshine, then a lily, a bouquet of myrrh and also a lyre—all these things in a dozen lines. St. Teresa adds that she will always hide herself in this face—

[6] Poems, p. 54.   [7] Poems, p. 10.

a conceit that appeals to her, for she repeats it twice at least in other poems! What did she mean exactly?

To us in England most of these poems are unbearably sentimental and sometimes do not seem to make sense. Take, if you like, the poem, "The divine dew". At the end of the third stanza the dew becomes milk: "Thy sweet Sun [of Jesus] is the breast of Mary and thy dew is the virginal milk."[8] In the next three verses, the divine blood, then the bread of the angels, and last "*ma blanche Hostie*" become all of them "the virginal milk". This may be suitable literature for some. May we say that we consider it unsuitable for general consumption?

Let us insist that these criticisms are not aimed at St. Teresa, but at her ill-advised admirers. As a tyro she was entitled to these *juvenilia*, but some at least of her poems might have been spared injudicious praise and an unnecessary publication.

* * *

Both in the prose and the poems of St. Teresa a curious feature appears, which may perhaps be properly commented upon in an essay on her style and personality. It is a very unexpected one in such a strong-willed and practical woman as she was, yet very much in evidence in many pages of her writings. She likes to think and to speak of herself as a little child, and uses baby language. After the episode of the interview with Leo XIII, her biography offers us this symbol of herself: she is the toy of the child Jesus, a little ball for him to play with. Jesus acts as an irresponsible baby would, "takes up the ball, throws it down, rolls it far away or presses it to his heart". She wants to play, as a child, with the Infant Jesus. "*Afin de te ravir, je veux rester petite.*"[9] "I

---

[8] "*Ton doux soleil est le sein de Marie
Et ta rosée est le lait virginal
. . . . . .
Ton sang divin, c'est le lait virginal,*" etc.
[9] Poems, p. 28.

want to remain little that I may delight thee" for it is her joy to feel small and helpless.[10] She calls herself, "A little Flower", or even, "a poor little flower". She is a little bird: "I am a poor little bird just covered with a little down." When she is preparing for Communion she imagines herself to be a little child of three or four and Our Lady comes to make her ready by changing her pinafore, arranging her hair, and adorning it with a pretty ribbon.[11] She imagines the child Jesus playing ninepins with her and saying: "Let us change the game; ninepins amuse me greatly but I should like to play at spinning a top, etc." . . .[12]

All this may sound very childish, but, in order to understand it, we should remember that at home she had been "the baby" of a large family and, as such, spoilt by M. Martin, who was really a born grandfather. Perhaps on account of her breakdown and of her extreme sensitiveness she occupied a privileged position in the home and was spared everything in the nature of housework. She was very obedient to Pauline, but remained always, for them all, the youngest, the baby. Under the hard discipline of Carmel it is natural that Teresa's thoughts would turn innocently to those early days when, at every step, she was lovingly taken care of and saved from responsibilities. She longed to be a child again; she still thought of herself as one and dreamt of Jesus treating her like one. She spoke of herself to her sisters as a baby: "Leave it to Daddy, to God. He knows what His tiny little baby needs." "Are you a baby, then?" said Marie to her. "Yes," she answered, "only a baby who thinks a lot and who is very old in experience."[13] Such fancies as this may sound surprising but they are not uncommon. How often one hears some powerfully built middle-aged women speak of themselves as "Poor little me!" It is not at all certain that St. Teresa, as the Valiant woman—which she was—would have appealed very much to the simple multitudes. They prefer the sentimental picture of a young saint, childishly weak and helpless

---

[10] N.V., p. 20.   [11] E, p. 322.   [12] E, p. 320.
[13] Petitot, *Ste. Thérèse de Lisieux, edition définitives.*

and pathetic. The symbol of the real Teresa might be a sturdy oak tree. They prefer to call her by her own chosen designation: "The Little Flower."

*   *   *

To these remarks on her curious return to baby language and to the frame of mind that caused her to adopt it, we must add an important corrective, although it has nothing to do with style. It is this: when it came to giving practical decisions or advice she was full of common sense. During her last illness we have seen how sensibly she answered the foolish suggestions of some nuns about visions, transports of love, etc.

We have also noticed, in their time and place, her answers to such Sisters as wanted to follow in her footsteps either by spreading the doctrine of the Little Way, or writing their own biographies, or sending edifying letters to the clergy. She knew them to have more zeal than understanding. They might have turned her Little Way into a New Quietism, and their vanity more than the Kingdom of God would have been served by pious correspondence and sanctimonious autobiographies. She knew herself to be the exception and that the best rule for the others was obedience to St. Paul's injunction "*Taceant in Ecclesia mulieres*".